10/02

Smashing Glazes

Smashing Glazes

53 Artists Share Insights and Recipes

Susan Peterson

GUILD Publishing, Madison, Wisconsin
Distributed by North Light Books, Cincinnati, Ohio

SMASHING GLAZES
53 Artists Share Insights and Recipes

Susan Peterson

Design: Cheryl Smallwood-Roberts
Chief Editorial Officer: Katie Kazan

Published by
GUILD Publishing
An imprint of GUILD.com
931 East Main Street • Madison, WI 53703 USA
TEL 608-257-2590 • TEL 877-284-8453 • FAX 608-227-4179

Distributed to the trade and art markets in North America by
North Light Books
An imprint of F&W Publications, Inc.
1507 Dana Avenue • Cincinnati, OH 45207
TEL 800-289-0963

Printed in China

ISBN 1-893164-05-5

Front cover artwork: Tom Coleman, *Cobalt Treatment,* cone 6 stoneware teapot, 26" x 24" x 3".
Photo by O'Gara Photography. This image is also shown on the title page.

Back cover artwork: Marc Leuthold, *Purple Wheel,* 2000, cone 04 red earthenware, 6" diameter.
Photo by Eva Heyd.

**GUILD Publishing is an imprint of GUILD.com, which sells works of art on the Internet.
Visit us, day or night, at www.guild.com.**

CONTENTS

Introduction 7

Low Fire 13
Lucy Breslin
Nan Smith
Robert Milnes
Ron Kovatch
Judy Kogod
Joan Bruneau
Carol Rossman
Sandra Luehrsen
Richard Slee
Linda Huey
Nancy Selvin
Marc Leuthold
Vineet Kacker
Annabeth Rosen

Medium Fire 43
Sandra Black
Lynn Goodman
Linda Speranza
Tom Coleman
Anne Fallis Elliot
Bernardo Hogan
Pippin Drysdale
Victoria Shaw
Barbara Sorenson
Jeanne Otis
Virginia Scotchie

High Fire 67
Hwang Jeng-Daw
Hein Severijns
Val Cushing
Maria Ana Gutierrez
Gillian Hodge
Tapio Yli-Viikari
Cathi Jefferson
Jeroen Bechtold
Maria Bofill
Piet Stockmans
Fritz Rossman
Robert Pulley
Ray Meeker
Bai Ming
Greg Daly
Sequoia Miller

Alternative Surfaces 101
Greg Payce
Tjok Dessauvage
Jim Behan
Jeff Oestreich
Randy Johnston
Janet Mansfield
Mindy Moore
Barbara Nanning
Bruce Bangert
Rick Berman
Joan Takayama Ogawa
Matthew Castle

Glossary 127

ACKNOWLEDGMENTS

My thanks to all the artists who answered my call for beautiful glazes in preparation for this book. Much of ceramic art today involves the look of raw clay and unglazed colored engobe surfaces rather than traditional glaze finishes. Still, the nuances from matt and glossy surfaces do carry exciting visual experiences, as this book suggests.

I have necessarily edited each artist's account of process, technique and aesthetic evaluations in regard to the finishes on the selected work. I have also, in some cases, recalculated an artist's original "parts-by-weight" recipe into percentage amounts adding to 99 or 100 or 101, so that all the glazes can be easily compared with each other.

It is a fact that no two glazes will ever appear exactly alike, even when mixed with like materials and fired in similar conditions. No two circumstances are ever the same, even in the same backyard. The batches and results included here are interesting guides only. We must experiment with our own materials and make our own adjustments. Variation and surprise have always been implicit in the ceramic art form.

The artists in this book were chosen from the responses I received from a request I sent to the 1500 ceramists on my mailing list. I know many of these artists personally; others I have never met. It is always a rewarding experience for me to open their packages of slides and transparencies.

Where the artist gave another artist's name to a glaze, or attributed a glaze's beginnings to someone else, I have included the name. However, most of us begin somewhere with somebody else's batch. Only so many elements that can be used in ceramic glazes exist on earth; depending on the temperature, most glazes for similar looks carry similar ingredients. For this reason, I believe that no glazes are really "secret" or "owned." Today we all share.

My gratitude is due to Katie Kazan, chief editorial officer at GUILD.com, who packaged this book, and to my assistant, Lucy Horner, as well as to all others who are engaged in my life and contribute to my daily pursuits. I hope you will all keep in touch.

Susan Peterson

INTRODUCTION

The history of glaze is a fascinating story of one of man's most wondrous accidental and intuitive discoveries. And because of the hand-in-glove relationship of clay and glaze, the history of one cannot be told except in tandem with the other.

Ceramic engineers have been known to say that ceramics was the world's first science, but the term "ceramics" has had varied meanings over the centuries. Before the space age we categorized a ceramic object as one where silica was the major molecular component of a piece fired to at least red heat — that is, to bonfire temperature of 1300°F (700°C) or above. With 20th-century outer

The author's updraft gas kiln.

space exploration, extreme temperatures became commonplace, and today the term has broadened to mean the use of refractory (very high firing) elements on the chemistry table that are shaped and processed alone or in combinations in temperatures up to 10,000°F (5540°C). This extreme temperature is far above the heat required for conventional clay or glaze, and artists and industry still fire dinnerware, art ware and sculpture from about 1800°F to 2400°F (982°C to

1320°C). Most ceramic materials are the highest firing among all the elements on the earth.

The Geography of Ceramics

Natural clays exist all over the world and fit geologically into five categories: china clays (also called kaolins), ball clays, stoneware clays, fireclays and common surface clays. Thus anyone anywhere has access to the same basic types of clays. Similarly, the basic minerals from which glazes are made are found almost everywhere in the world.

Ceramic materials are the only ones on the face of the earth that withstand fires, freezing, water damage and the like and — when properly fired — can never alter. We study ancient man through the ceramic artifacts excavated from bygone civilizations. As well, the next generation will go to the moon in a glazed pot, although it will be made of more esoteric materials than clay and glaze.

Back down to earth, clay — an alteration product of original igneous rock — has existed since the beginning of time and will continuously form until the end of the world. Primitive man made and bonfired clay pots decorated only with metallic oxides and other colored clays for at least 35,000 years. Certain cultures still do so today, notably in Africa, India and the American Southwest.

Glass was discovered, we think, by the Egyptians in approximately 5000 B.C. Probably an accidental combination of salt and sand in just the right proportions caused shimmering glassy globules to be found in the ashes of an open cooking fire. Later, man learned to shape molten glass by cast or blow-pipe methods once the basic elements of sand, salt and fire were understood. Silica — found in sand — was the important mineral necessary for glass-forming chemistry, and soda — found in salt — acted as the flux to lower the temperature of more refractory silica. Eventually a powdery mixture of salt and sand was probably mixed with water and applied to a clay pot, resulting in a glassy coating during the fire.

As history elongated, kilns were built. Because they contained more heat than open fires, temperatures could be higher and varieties of clay bodies and glazes became possible. Regions of the world developed their own styles, generally from the materials and coloring oxides that were locally available.

The geology of China yielded an exceptional naturally combined deposit of pure china clay and feldspar, the true ingredients of a porcelain body. The Chinese used this for several thousand years before they learned to fire high enough for density (i.e., a nonporous fired clay) at around 1 A.D. Natural feldspathic china clay deposits were eventually located in Korea, Japan and India, but none have been found elsewhere in the world in amounts sufficient for mining. Europeans, having no natural china clay body to prospect, tried for centuries to make porcelain from various minerals. Finally, in the 18th century, the German chemist Johann Friedrich Bottger and the Englishman Josiah Wedgwood discovered, almost simultaneously, how to combine pure china clay and bone ash with other fluxes in correct proportions and to fire hot enough to achieve translucent porcelain.

In the United States, glazed ceramics have a short history, dating from 1620, when the first Pilgrims arrived on the eastern seaboard. Many early settlers were potters from Europe. In the western United States, settled primarily by Spanish and inhabited by native Indians, a low-fire earthenware culture existed for several centuries before stoneware and porcelain migrated from the east.

European glazed ceramics had been influenced by Mesopotamian earthenware from the Middle Ages, which was decorated with colored clay engobes and clear glaze, as well as by the functional peasant pottery that existed in central Europe from the first century A.D. The advent of porcelain in Europe after 1750 resulted in unprecedented technical virtuosity in both low and high fire, epitomized by the flamboyant designs of the Victorian era. In contrast, the art of Far Eastern ceramics has remained classically sophisticated in style to this day.

Today, mass-production ceramics has become the workhorse of space-age technology. Computer chips, sewing machine parts, jet engine units, machine tools, nose cones for rockets and spaceships, under water vehicles, et cetera, comprise the new output. We are living in the age of ceramics, no longer in the age of metals.

Kilns and Firing

Earthenware temperature ranges, from approximately 1800°F to 2000°F (982°C to 1090°C), are familiar to us in products like brick and flowerpots. Artists often work within this temperature range when making sculpture, since the work remains porous and light in weight, does not shrink much in drying and firing, and has vivid and varied glaze color possibilities. Stoneware pieces, usually fired from 2000°F to 2200°F (1090°C to 1200°C), are more dense, more durable and heavier, with somewhat muted colors as temperatures go higher. Porcelain, which is usually white and can be translucent if thin, is the most dense, most durable, and generally the highest firing in the vocabulary of the ceramic artist.

Early firing chambers, now called kilns, were probably

caves where the enclosed walls could contain heat, allowing for higher temperatures than open fires. The first kilns in China and Japan were built on an incline, with single chambers or multiple sections; these "climbing" or "dragon" kilns have the firebox at the low end and the flue at the high end. In the Western world the first kilns were brick structures where fire from wood or gas underneath the ware surrounded it with a heated atmosphere that moved up through the pots and out a small flue opening at the top; these are called "updraft" kilns. Later, "downdraft" kilns, with a flue opening at the back of the chamber, were devised. Theoretically, this arrangement facilitates more even temperatures inside the kiln, although updraft kilns can fire much faster. Electric-element kilns were initially built in countries where petroleum fuels did not exist, but today are used by artists everywhere. Electricity does not permit a change of atmosphere from fully oxidizing to partially oxidizing; this latter atmosphere, called "reduction," makes possible the Sung dynasty Chinese colors of oxblood red and celadon green, as well as rust-black oil-spot glazes.

The great unglazed clay sculptures of ancient Chinese and Japanese temples, the clay horses and warriors of the Xian tombs and the huge ceremonial Ayyanaur horses of India were doubtless fired by building huge brick or clay walls around the figures, enclosing the fire. The kilns were dismantled to extract the sculptures. Artists today are exploring all the old types of kilns — including salt-glaze and wood fire, pit-firings, sawdust firing in saggers, garbage firings and raku firings — as well as unusual kiln designs for specific results. Firing processes, temperatures and atmospheres, as well as different types of kilns, go hand in hand with the creative aspects of glazing.

After ceramic work has been fabricated and dried at room temperature, it is usually given a preliminary firing to harden the ware enough to be handled during decorating and glazing. This initial firing, accomplished at about 1600°F to 1800°F (871°C to 982°C), is called a "bisque" or "biscuit" firing. When the kiln is cool, the ware is removed for glaze application. Some cultures, some artists, and many commercial factories apply glaze to raw ware and "once-fire" for reasons of economy or artistic effect.

Glazes and Glazing

Glaze does not make the fired clay pot dense or leakproof. Glaze is merely a coating over the clay body. It is used to achieve color and decorative patterns with a shiny or matt surface that is easily cleaned and quite sanitary.

Glazes are initially mixed dry from a variety of minerals based on percentage combinations for the different temperature ranges of earthenware, stoneware and porcelain; in use, water is added to the dry mix until it's the consistency of light cream. At low fire, the usual flux for the necessary glass-forming ingredient — silica — may be in the form of ground glass, a commercial "frit" (a prefired and reground low-melting combination of ceramic materials), or very low-melting materials such as lead, soda or boric acid. At medium to high fire, the usual flux is a feldspar (soda, potassium or calcium). Compounding glazes for desired surfaces, colors and heat treatments is a complex science in itself. Artists learn to master the chemistry of glazes, or they trade recipes with each other, find glaze batches in books, or buy glazes manufactured commercially.

Glaze combinations, mixed liquid with water, should ideally be stored in hardwood or stoneware containers, but most artists use plastic buckets with lids. Commercial glazes are typically sold liquid in four-ounce jars, but they have a very short (several-month) shelf life and deteriorate quickly. Alternatively, commercial glazes can be purchased dry-mixed in larger quantities. One pound of dry glaze will yield approximately one pint of liquid glaze; about eight pounds of dry glaze will yield one gallon of liquid glaze; 454 grams equals one pound.

Experimentation and documentation are important in developing glazes. No two glazes of the same batch will fire the same in different kilns, with different fuels, in different places or at different altitudes. Usually a glaze recipe must be adapted to new circumstances by altering the ingredients or by changing the firing procedure. Raw materials vary in every steam-shovel load at the mine. For accuracy, glaze tests or individual material tests should be made of new or substitute ingredients, and as much as possible brand names and vendors should not be substituted.

Glaze application is as important as proper firing. Normal glaze thickness is $1/32$ of an inch (.08 centimeter). Thinner or thicker application than normal will provide a different look. Many matt glazes will gloss if they are too thin; most glazes will crawl or fall off the pot during firing if the application is too thick. Overlays of application will result in pattern definition, and most application techniques will show. Brushing should be used only when you want the rhythm of the brush mark; pouring yields an even application if the pouring is even, but not if there are drips or overlaps; spraying, which *should* be the easiest way to accomplish an even glaze coat, is even only when actually sprayed evenly.

Color and Design

Decorating — sometimes called "pattern making" — can be accomplished by using white or colored engobes under a glaze. An engobe is a basic white clay or clay body, mixed with water to the proper consistency for the desired application treatment; for color, it can be mixed with additions of 10% to 50% of various metallic oxides that withstand high temperatures. Commonly used oxides are iron (for amber to brown), manganese (purple-brown), vanadium (yellow), rutile (orange), cobalt (blue), copper (grass green) and nickel (gray). Engobes are usually applied to wet or leather-hard clay and can be drawn through in the method known as "sgraffito." Special engobe formulations are possible for coating bisqued ware. Engobes are brushed, sprayed, sponged or poured in thicknesses similar to oil paints, and engobe designs can be covered with clear glossy or translucent matt glazes, or left unglazed. Wax resists and stencils can also be used for pattern making. "Slip-trailed" decoration is done by squeezing engobes through a plastic applicator or syringe.

Metallic oxides can be used alone for ornament, with or without glaze. Mixed with water, coloring oxides are painted on, much like watercolors. The method of oxide decoration used under a glaze is called "underglaze decoration"; the technique of applying oxide decoration over glazes is called "majolica" and is reminiscent of a traditional Italian technique.

The oxide color palette is broadened by manufactured stains. These ceramic colorants are made from basic metallic oxides combined with other ingredients to yield a wider range of color. Commercial manufacturers also make engobes, but call them "underglazes" or "one strokes," and they compound stain mixtures without fluxes, calling them "overglazes." Underglaze pencils, watercolor tubes, trailing bottles, and spray jars are also sold; all are filled with ceramic pigments of various sorts.

Glazes are colored by adding the same metallic oxides used in coloring clay engobes, but in percentages from 2% to 15% added to 100% of base glaze. Some glaze colors, such as fire-engine red, orange, and bright yellow, can be accomplished best in the low temperature range, and are almost always bought commercially made, as are luster glazes and golds.

See-through, transparent and translucent glazes are usually applied over engobes. Colored opaque glazes can coat red, buff or white clay and will probably obliterate underglaze decoration. Colored clay bodies influence the true color of a glaze coating, while white clay undergrounds enhance the pure color of any given glaze. The same metallic oxides used in engobes can be used to color clear or opaque white base glazes, but when the color is saturated in a glaze, it is usually stronger and richer than can be obtained in engobe decoration.

Some coloring oxides change depending upon the atmosphere in which they're fired. One-half to one percent iron oxide added to a glaze, for instance, will ordinarily produce an amber-yellow in oxidation and a sea-green celadon color in reduction. Similar tiny amounts of copper oxide will give turquoise in oxidation but a Chinese oxblood red in reduction.

In order to duplicate any results, artists must keep accurate records of glazes — including materials and brand names — as well as exact firing charts. To accomplish this, a temperature gauge — called a pyrometer — must be used to monitor the firings, with the exact heat inside the kiln measured with a thermocouple. Although a pyrometer-thermocouple device is the only efficient way to measure the progress of a kiln firing, it's important to still monitor the kiln with pyrometric cones (small, elongated pyramids of clay and glaze constituents that soften and bend at specific temperatures). No cones or pyrometers are accurate in salt or wood firings, so draw trials (small rings of clay that can be pulled from the kiln to test the temperature) are a better solution.

Glazes can be mathematically calculated from molecular formulas, or batches (sometimes called "recipes") can be changed into molecular formulas, in order to be very specifically altered. The calculation process is well explained in my book *The Craft and Art of Clay* (3rd edition). Computer programs are available to do the mathematical calculation, but even with this modern convenience, glaze testing and strict documentation of procedures are essential in each distinct environment.

Most professional potters prefer the term "batch" when referring to a glaze mixture. The batch should always add up to 100 parts, so that any amount needed can be computed easily. Color is almost always an addition to the 100% batch, as are texture enhancements such as sand and grog. By the same token, clay body batches should add to 100%; again, any colorant or texture enhancement would be an addition. Most clay bodies are weighed in pounds; most glazes are weighed in grams. Scales are only as accurate as the money you pay for them. Volume measurements are acceptable if the same measures are always used, but volume does not translate to weight. The most pertinent advice is to be consistent.

Glaze batches are listed in organized fashion, so as to be compared easily with other glazes. Usually the material with the largest percentage is listed first. Alternately, the frit or feldspar may be listed first, although generally one of those two *is* the largest amount in a glaze. Other materials come next, in order of amount, except that clay and silica amounts are listed last in the batch. Most glazes are 50% silica, with the silica supplied through several different materials, including frit, feldspar, talc and clay, to name a few. Clay is added in glazes for suspension and application reasons. Most glazes contain 10% china or ball clay (ball clay suspends best and is less refractory, but china clay is whiter) and 10% pure silica, the last two ingredients to be listed in the batch. As stated, col-

orants and opacifiers are usually percentage additions to the 100% batch.

Suspension agents can be added to glaze to keep the consistency even and for ease of application. Bentonite is a type of clay that is often an addition or an ingredient in old-fashioned glaze batches. I do not recommend its use because it tends to expand when mixed with water and then shrink excessively on drying; this can cause crawling or flaking. Epsom salts, Calgon (dishwasher detergent), organic gums such as tragacanth and arabic, and synthetic gums such as methocelullose (CMC) are better choices for suspending glazes. One percent magnesium carbonate is a good choice for an addition to a dry or wet batch to help the liquid suspension.

Reasons for making your own glaze instead of buying a commercial mixture are many. Commercial batches are secret, whereas your own is your own to be altered or modified. Making your own glaze is also much cheaper than purchasing commercial mixtures. And commercial mixes include synthetic additions that hold them in suspension but lessen their shelf life.

Substitutions are possible when ingredients are of similar composition. Analyses of complex materials are available in *The Craft and Art of Clay* and many other books. Many frits, no matter the composition, will substitute one for another. Feldspars substitute generally, but one must know the molecular formula to substitute specifically. Certain oxides are necessary for certain glaze colors, therefore substitutes may change the color. The only way to find out if something works is to test it.

Glazes are given names for peculiar reasons. Some glazes are famous and have been used for generations, some glazes are passed around under different names but are in fact the same, and some glazes are altered from the original even if the so-called name is the same. Most artists feel it is best to compound their own glazes from their own material sources; even if every ingredient is essentially the same, the results will almost inevitably be different in another location, in another kiln. It's even common to have difficulty duplicating your own results!

Safety

It almost goes without saying that safety precautions should be taken when mixing chemicals. You should work in a well-ventilated room — preferably with windows open — or outside in the air. It's wise to wear surgical gloves when mixing glazes, and a mask to prevent breathing dust. Raw lead and several other chemicals are avoided these days; you will probably encounter them only in manufactured frits, which have been prefired to high enough temperatures to become non-poisonous and insoluble. If you are working with lusters, china paints or enamels, it's especially important to wear a mask and gloves.

When firing electric kilns, do not touch elements with wet hands or feet, and try to have a rubber mat in front of your kiln to stand on. With gas or other fueled kilns, all fire hazards must be removed from the kiln area during firing. No kiln, no matter what its fuel, should ever be left alone during the time of firing, even for a few minutes. Never light the burners to start a firing on a closed-up gas kiln; always have the door or lid open and peepholes out. If burners on a gas kiln should blow out, do not relight them without opening up the kiln. When throwing wood or salt into a kiln, beware of backpressure, and never stand directly in front of the firebox or stoke hole.

Glaze batches from books, ceramic classes or the Internet are a good place to start experimenting, but these glazes can serve only as basic beginnings for your own development in your own circumstance. *Smashing Glazes* has great value in the reports of individual artists' glazes and techniques, but it is best used as a springboard. Even more important — for collectors and ceramists — is to understand these artists' thought processes, with particular emphasis on how they think about and develop their ceramic surfaces.

This book is unique for the reason that these artists have made the effort to describe their analyses, their clay and glaze formulations, and their own dreams and concepts about ceramic art.

NOTE
Throughout *Smashing Glazes,* dimensions are given in inches.
To convert to centimeters, multiply by 2.54.

LOW FIRE

Lucy Breslin

Nan Smith

Robert Milnes

Ron Kovatch

Judy Kogod

Joan Bruneau

Carol Rossman

Sandra Luehrsen

Richard Slee

Linda Huey

Nancy Selvin

Marc Leuthold

Vineet Kacker

Annabeth Rosen

LUCY BRESLIN

UNITED STATES

I use an eclectic mix of glazes and processes, mostly on hand-built pieces. I develop my own glazes or adjust borrowed ones, but I vary this with commercial glazes too.

I like to spray the White Matt over the whole piece, then brush bright colors in special areas. I may cover some areas with liquid latex resist, then spray over the whole surface with Oops Revised, with or without added color. Usually two or three glazes are applied in varying amounts, in two and three layers. By using more than one glaze and various layers, I'm able to create a visual depth and increase the richness. Last, I sometimes brush small amounts of prepared glazes over some sprayed areas to create even greater depth.

The liquid latex resist must be removed before firing. It's unlike wax in that if latex is left on during firing, those areas will turn a murky brown.

It takes me several hours to glaze a piece; less time-consuming methods have not yielded good results. So much comes from visualizing previous experience. I spend a lot of time gardening and receive much pleasure from the way color works in nature. My intent is not to copy nature, but to make color bountiful in my own work.

Another goal in my glazing is for the piece to regather some of the vitality present during the form-making with wet clay. For me, a bisqued pot is lifeless. Glazing brings it back to life.

CLAY BODY
White earthenware: AP Green fireclay 35%, china clay 25%, ball clay 25%, frit (3124) 10%, sand 5%.

GLAZES
White Matt: barium carbonate 6%, lithium carbonate 10%, whiting 9%, zinc oxide 10%, china clay 22%, silica 42%, bentonite 1%.

Oops Revised: frit (3124) 42%, lithium carbonate 7%, whiting 14%, china clay 15%, silica 20%, bentonite 2%. For blue, add 4% copper carbonate; for other colors, add 3% to 8% Mason stains.

FIRING
Electric kiln, cone 04 (1940°F/1060°C).

Lucy Breslin, *Blue Bowl for Red Apples,* cone 04 earthenware, 9" x 17" x 11". Photo by Mark Johnson.

NAN SMITH

UNITED STATES

For my sculptures I desire a soft, graduated coloration that embodies subtlety, realism, transparency and the idea of light projecting onto a surface. Some of the color seems to emanate from within, as does the floral shadow on the chest of the twin figures in this work. I feel that brush strokes destroy the purity I seek in the illusion. Airbrush and commercial underglaze color provide the vehicle and media to create a painterly effect, but give the varied texture and color richness of layered glaze.

I use two crawl glazes over commercial underglazes. I spray six to ten coats of underglaze color, depending on the hue and its intensity. I apply highlights with the airbrush. Sometimes I cut paper stencils by hand, using small scissors like those in traditional Chinese paper cutting. The floral elements were sprayed with a base coating of white stain under the yellow.

A computer programmer and I carefully monitor the firing for each sculpture. I fire the kiln up and down slowly. Electricity gives me control of the cycle, and the glaze colors remain pure and bright in the oxidation atmosphere.

CLAY BODY

Buff earthenware for sculpture: fireclay 18%, Goldart 24%, local clay 8%, talc 10%, fine sand 20%, fine grog 20%.

GLAZES

Crawl Base: borax 4%, Gerstley borate 47%, magnesium carbonate 31%, china clay 19%.

Shin Li's Good Crawl: frit (3195) 50%, magnesium carbonate 30%, china clay 20%.

FIRING

Electric kiln, cone 03 (2014°F/1101°C) oxidation.

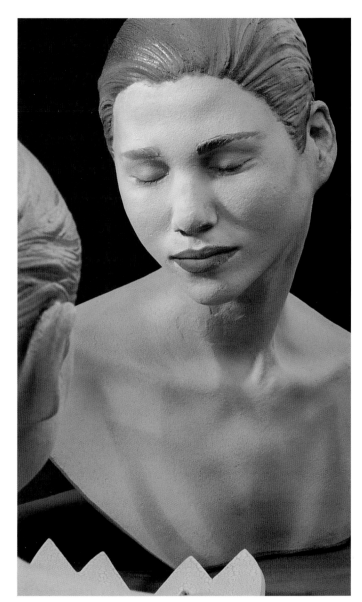

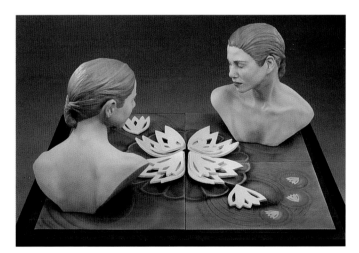

Nan Smith, *Oneness,* 1999, cone 03 airbrushed, glazed earthenware on a wooden pedestal, 54³/₄" x 34¹/₂" x 40¹/₄". Photos by Allen Chevron.

ROBERT MILNES

UNITED STATES

These pieces are built from slabs that are assembled like coils. I build the heads as a complete half-dome and add the features using slabs of clay for the nose, ears and so on. *Clearly* is based on the shape of an *edamane* (a Japanese soybean) and a sculpture by Constantin Brancusi. The back of the piece has a quotation from Ludwig Wittgenstein in Morse code: "Everything that can be thought can be thought clearly."

The slips and glazes are based on gentle color combinations. *Clearly* uses a yellow slip under a heavy application of Pale Turquoise Crawl with accents of maroon. The eye pupils are covered with engobe, plus 15% Mason Black Stain 6600, and a commercial low-fire clear glaze. The eyes have an illusory limpid look and they do follow you around the room. After the first firing to cone 04, I might add more glaze and refire several more times to cone 04.

Much of my newest sculpture carries Morse code. One of the first modern languages, it's now officially dead, put away by the Internet, new communication forms, and English as the international language. I like Morse code's abstract, binary and geometric character. Ludwig Wittgenstein's book *Tractatus Logico-Philosophicus* is one of the classic texts of modern philosophy.

CLAY BODY
White earthenware: talc 40%, fireclay 20%, ball clay 40%.

GLAZES
Burkett Crawl: Gerstley borate 47%, magnesium carbonate 31%, borax 4%, china clay 19%.

Variation #1
Pale Turquoise: add 12% Mason stain 6288.

Variation #2
Turquoise Gray: add 6% Mason stain 6390 and 6% Mason stain 6500.

Roloff Satin: Gerstley borate 38%, lithium carbonate 10%, nepheline syenite 7%, china clay 5%, silica 40%.

Variation
Maroon: add 12% Mason stain 6065.

ENGOBE
Vitreous engobe: Gerstley borate 25%, borax 6.25%, Zircopax 6.25%, china clay 18.75%, ball clay 18.75%, silica 25%. Add Mason stains 12 to 15%.

FIRING
Electric kiln, cone 04 (1940°F/1060°C) oxidation.

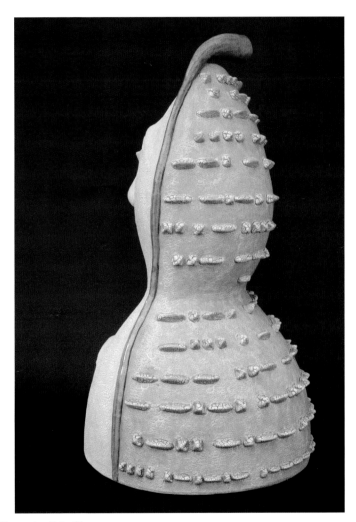

Robert Milnes, *Clearly,* 1999, cone 04 earthenware, 27" x 15$^{1}/_{2}$" x 17$^{1}/_{2}$". Photos by Kyle Chesser.

RON KOVATCH

UNITED STATES

This glaze has an Egyptian paste quality of luminescence that I love. Use it thick: if the glaze is thinner, the color is more transparent. If you use it over red clay the iron in the body mutes the electricity of the blue.

I handbuild with coils in a simple technique. The sperm-like surface of this piece is made with thousands of one-inch-long conical shapes formed by hand and applied to the leather-hard surface of the head as it is constructed.

I spice up the clay body by including in the mix varying amounts of floor sweepings. I like the clay coarse, but it makes it difficult to work. For some perverse reason I think art should challenge the mental as well as the physical.

Sometimes I discover a glaze and make a piece with that glaze in mind. I spend one month testing hundreds of glazes before doing a new body of work. That is how I worked *Te Amo*. This glaze from my tests looked like water. It had a visceral quality that I wanted to use to reinforce the slick cartoon-like sexuality of this piece. Normally I hate blue glazes since they seem so commercial, and yet some of that quality is exactly what I wanted here. I wanted lurid, loud colors and surfaces that, although they have subtleties, are garish, vibrating and magnetic.

I love texture: busy, historied, aggressive texture with fingerprints, tool marks, irregularity, pattern, mistakes, erasures.

CLAY BODY
White earthenware, plus grog or silica sand to taste.

GLAZE
Turquoise Blue: baking soda 30.5%, lithium carbonate 8.5%, china clay 22.5%, silica 38.5%. Add 10% Zircopax, 2.5% copper carbonate.

FIRING
Electric kiln, cone 04 (1940°F/1060°C) oxidation.

Ron Kovatch, *Te Amo,* cone 04 white earthenware, 24" x 10" x 10". Photo by Wimer Zehr.

JUDY KOGOD

UNITED STATES

I decorate my slab-built pieces in the leather-hard stage with colored engobes — liquid combinations of clay and small amounts of other ingredients, plus pigments. My clay body fires white, so first I paint the areas I want to remain white — like the leaves on the trays and the melons on the vase — with liquid latex resist. Then I brush on three coats of the background colors. I may scratch lines through the latex and inlay color. After I peel off the resist, I can further define shapes or add drawings with lines by slip-trailing and incising. I like the essence of the brushed-on, thick quality of the clay engobe, which is opaque, like oil paint.

Everything is bisque fired slowly 12 to 14 hours. Then the clear glaze is applied and the work is refired slowly for another 12 to 14 hours.

I am interested in color, pattern and movement. I love the way many patterns together create something greater than the sum of their parts. I can't say exactly why I like some patterns on some shapes. I just play around in an intuitive way until I am satisfied.

CLAY BODY
Talc body earthenware.

ENGOBE
White Slip: ball clay 40%, china clay 20%, frit (3124) 10%, nepheline syenite 15%, talc 15%. For red, add Amaco liquid underglaze Maroon 56; for other colors, add Mason stains by eye.

GLAZE
Cushing Clear Gloss: frit (3124) 30%, Gerstley borate 26%, nepheline syenite 20%, lithium carbonate 4%, china clay 10%, silica 10%.

FIRING
Electric kiln, cone 04 (1940°F/1060°C).

Judy Kogod, *Melon Vase,* cone 04 earthenware, 14" x 5" x 2". Photo by PRS Associates.

JOAN BRUNEAU
CANADA

My work is influenced by botanical structures, landscape, and ceramic history. I choose glaze colors and textures, as well as opaque and translucent qualities, to recall visual and tactile experiences and restate meanings conveyed in the forms. I like juxtaposing opacity and translucency, shiny and matt, and sometimes glaze versus exposed clay body.

Most glazes are best applied by dipping and pouring to ensure consistent coverage. I brush glazes on smaller areas such as handles. Deb's Base with colorants and Zaeder's Matt, when overlapped thick, can run. That tendency is the beauty of these glazes — just be careful. I "soak" (hold the temperature) on both bisque and glaze firings for 20 to 40 minutes at the end to let the gases escape and avoid pinholes in the glaze.

The glaze firing to cone 04 takes about nine hours. I put Orton cone packs with cones 06, 05, 04 and 03 at the peepholes and adjust the switches on the electric kiln to keep the temperature even inside the kiln.

My well-insulated kiln takes 24 hours to cool to room temperature. I cool slowly to prevent crazing and dunting. The addition to the clay body of up to 10% kyanite (an aluminosilicate with high resistance to thermal shock), 100-mesh particle size, also reduces the possibility of dunting.

CLAY BODY

Red earthenware: prospected clay 60%, Redart 10%, ball clay 15%, china clay 15%. Add 1% barium carbonate.

GLAZES

Zaeder Matt Lime (teapot neck): frit (3134) 40%, lithium carbonate 7%, wollastonite 25%, ball clay 22%, silica 6%. Add 7% Mason nickel silicate stain.

John's Revised Base Plum (teapot shoulder): frit (3110) 63%, frit (3124) 9%, Gerstley borate 10%, china clay 7%, silica 11%. Add 5% Mason Blackberry Wine Stain, 2% manganese carbonate, 0.25% cobalt.

Deb's Base (teapot body): frit (3134) 30%, frit (3195) 45%, china clay 25%.

Variations

Honey: add 7% burnt umber.

Moss: add 5% copper carbonate and 4% burnt umber.

FIRING

Electric kiln, cone 04 (1940°F/1060°C).

Joan Bruneau, untitled, 1998, cone 04 earthenware teapot, 8"H. Photo by Joan Bruneau.

CAROL ROSSMAN

CANADA

The thrown vessel was burnished in the leather-hard stage by polishing with wooden and rubber ribs. When bone dry, I apply terra sigillata with a wide, thick, natural brush in no more than two applications. All fine outlines are painted with Alligator. The pot is then buffed with a soft cloth and burnished again using stones and expired credit cards, then bisqued to cone 08.

The areas not to be glazed are masked off using graphic tapes. These parts will eventually be black and shiny after the post-firing reduction. I divided this vessel into thirds and used a pencil to rough in a pattern. Then I brushed Rossman's Burgundy Sheen and Reynold's Rap glazes where I needed those colors. Copper Sand and Blue Velvet were airbrushed over the entire piece, followed by a light spraying of Burgundy Sheen. After glazing, all graphic tapes were removed.

The pot was fired in a gas kiln to cone 08, removed, and immediately reduced. A bed of sawdust is prepared in a metal bin with a good lid to create a soft, solid base. A layer of newspaper is placed on the sawdust and a block of wood placed in the center. The sides are lined with *The New York Times*.

When the piece is removed from the kiln, it is placed immediately on the wood. When the flame is well established, the bin is covered. You can usually hear a little burp — a pop under the lid — once the smoke has subsided. The pot remains in the bin until it is cool. The arch on which the vessel stands is smoked.

The imagery on this piece came from my observing the intricate designs produced by the eddies in the Ottawa River, as the patterns wind and unwind in the flowing dark water.

CLAY BODY
Commercial raku clay.

GLAZES
Blue Velvet: by volume, bone ash 1 cup, Gerstley borate 3 cups, ball clay 1 cup, copper carbonate 1 cup, tin oxide $^1/_8$ cup, cobalt oxide 1 tablespoon.

Dry Burgundy Matt: Gerstley borate 50%, nepheline syenite 20%, talc 30%. Add 3% copper carbonate.

Rossman's Burgundy Sheen: Gerstley borate 55%, nepheline syenite 22.5%, talc 22.5%. Add 3% copper carbonate.

Alligator: bone ash 25%, Gerstley borate 50%, nepheline syenite 12.5%, copper carbonate 12.5%.

Reynold's Rap: barium carbonate 6%, Gerstley borate 64%, Custer feldspar 12%, ball clay 6%, silica 12%. Add 12% copper carbonate.

Copper Sand: by volume, Gerstley borate 8 cups, bone ash 2 cups, copper carbonate $^1/_2$ cup, cobalt oxide $^1/_4$ cup, tin oxide $^1/_8$ cup.

TERRA SIGILLATA
China clay 1755 grams, ball clay 405 grams, bentonite 90 grams, Calgon 11 grams. Add 21 cups water.

FIRING
Electric kiln for bisque, propane gas for raku, cone 08 (1751°F/955°C), post-firing reduction.

Carol Rossman, *Eddies,* cone 08 raku-fired pot on smoke-fired clay arch, 9" x 6¹/₂". Photo by Michael Dismatsek.

SANDRA LUEHRSEN

I use this matt glaze on my red clay sculptural vessels. Typically I cover the main body of the piece with the glaze and add colors to the decorative elements at the end of the Nichrome wires. The wires are applied to the raw clay from the beginning, then the accessories are added and then all are fired together, through the bisque kiln and the glaze kiln.

This glaze melts to a creamy surface with a mottled appearance. I add 10 percent Mason, Drakenfeld or Degussa stains to the glaze for each color. Some stains mottle more than others, and I haven't figured out why. Saturated chrome stains do not mix well with this glaze. Here I'm using Mason Avocado Green Stain with Mason Dark Teal and Sandstone.

The glaze should be applied thickly. I brush on three or four layers and sometimes add more glaze in a refire. The thicker the glaze, the creamier it is. This glaze will pool in crevices to enhance carved or applied decoration.

I created *Friends* for a summer bug show at a gallery. I wanted this to be a friendly, rather than a creepy, piece. My Avocado Green Matt covers the overall body of the piece, and I used brown accents at the top and bottom. The soft green represents the home where my bugs live. I use bright floral tone glazes for the bugs, so that the bugs appear unreal. Gold lusters were applied to the feelers in a third firing.

Sharp Nichrome wires penetrated my earliest heart sculptures. These works conveyed a sense of suffering that is not present in my current work. Later I began putting beads and flowers on the Nichrome wires and the mood of the work changed dramatically. Peace, and even whimsy, characterize these works now. I tend to use just a few glazes. I find that staying with a few selections reduces compatibility problems.

CLAY BODY
Commercial red earthenware.

GLAZES
Semi-Matt Alkaline: Gerstley borate 38%, lithium carbonate 10%, nepheline syenite 5%, china clay 5%, silica 42%. Add 10% stains.

FIRING
Electric kiln, cone 06 (1830°F/999°C).

Sandra Luehrsen, *Friends,* 1999, cone 06 earthenware with Nichrome wire,
15" x 12" x 11". Photo by Sandra Luehrsen.

RICHARD SLEE

GREAT BRITAIN

My feeling is that all ceramics should be shiny and reflective. I work in collections, around a central theme. Often it seems to me to be almost a bargain sale of objects held together by their common craft or stylistic qualities. They are models with a history of romance and sentimentality. The world I create is the landscape of the imagination, a fantasy that is both comforting and anxious. The sun always shines; the lights never go out.

For *Tents,* I used stains I buy in Britain — similar to those available elsewhere — called Azure Blue, Canary Yellow, Rosso Red, Lavender, Lilac, Maize Yellow and Grass Green. I use 36 different stain colors. Most of my pieces are multi-fired, layering one glaze over another. I do not keep records. I work intuitively and with some risk. If I have a philosophy it is that "all glazes should be shiny."

I work in two ways. Either color is determined by the subject matter of the piece, or the piece is determined by the glaze color and its qualities. The aim is to emotionally integrate form, surface and color into an object that is whole and familiar. Concave and convex surfaces will alter, weaken or intensify the color. By layering colored glazes, a depth of surface is given to that piece. Finally, however, this is all intuitive.

CLAY BODY
White earthenware: ball clay, cristobalite, dolomite.

GLAZE
Low-fire commercial clear glaze 85%, high alkaline frit 8%, china clay 7%. Add 7% or more of any glaze stains; for white, add 8% tin oxide.

FIRING
Electric kiln, cone 05 (1915°F/1046°C) oxidation.

Richard Slee, *Tents,* 2000, cone 05 earthenware, up to 6" high.

LINDA HUEY
UNITED STATES

I am interested in seedpods because of their close connection to both growth and decay. This craggy, cracked, cryolite glaze adds to the feeling.

I formed clay slabs over a steel armature so that the clay would shrink and crack over the metal in an interesting way. The glaze was applied in different thicknesses by stippling it on with a brush in a dabbing motion; this gives variation in color and texture. Inside the seedpod is a large metal coil that was added after the firing.

Dead flowers become seedpods that crack and decay in order to release the seed of new life. When a seedpod is made out of clay over metal, the resulting cracks also suggest a clash of the natural and the man-made. The dry matt glaze enhances the clashes.

I enjoy the risk of not being able to completely control the process of cracking in my clay pods, and the random cracking in the glaze. However, once they are fired, the cracks do stay permanently in place.

It is important to get over the fear that clay might crack, and also the fear of nature because it can't be controlled. I want to get over the fear of the glaze too, but I want some fear to show.

I like glazes that change a lot from thick to thin; they let me get a lot of mileage out of one glaze on one piece.

CLAY BODY
Commercial red earthenware.

GLAZE
Michael Hagadorn's Cryolite Matt: cryolite 33%, frit (3195) 17%, soda ash 17%, china clay 33%. Add 6% chrome oxide.

FIRING
Electric kiln cone 04 (1940°F/1060°C).

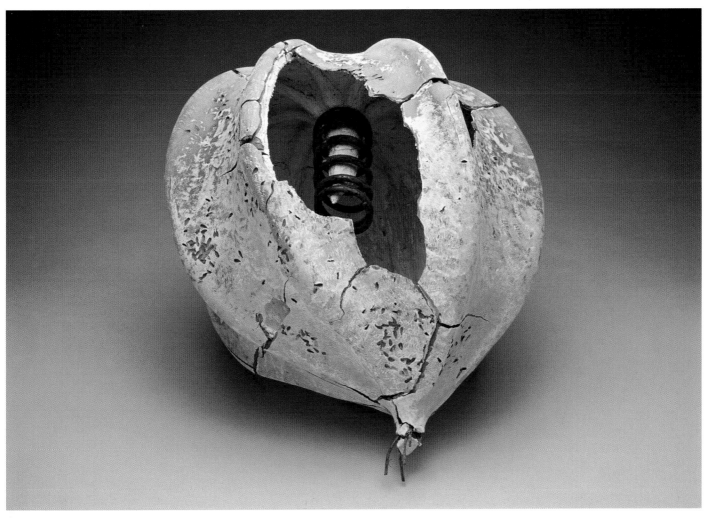

Linda Huey, *Seed Pod with Coil,* cone 04 earthenware, 20" x 20" x 20". Photo by M.J. Castle Studios.

NANCY SELVIN

UNITED STATES

I carved two solid models from sliced lumps of clay, two variations of a rice bowl form, from which four-piece plaster molds were made of each bowl. The multi-piece molds that create the inside and outside shapes were slipcast with liquid white clay, so I could have multiples for an installation. The bowls were bisqued to cone 010.

My clear glaze was poured about postcard thickness on the inside of each bowl and fired to cone 04. At this point the glazed interior and the unglazed exterior of the bowls are still pure white, one shiny, the other not shiny. This glaze works well in raku or with engobes showing through it, but I like to use commercial underglazes over it. In this case I sprayed Duncan Flame Red Underglaze over the fired shiny interior, and the effect was to matt the clear glaze. The unglazed exterior was sprayed with Duncan underglazes called Midnight Blue, Royal Blue-Green, Denim Blue, Teal and Cobalt Black, which I used near the top edge for definition. I stilted the bowls and fired everything again to cone 06 in the electric kiln.

I did a series of rice bowls airbrushed in different colors on lacquer trays. The faceted forms contrast with the thin casts and intense color. I made rice bowls to explore a more angular, irregular form with a sense of drama. Although they aren't really indigenous in my culture, they serve as a metaphor. For high contrast and something outstanding, I favor the unlikely pairing of color combinations.

The work appears simple but is in fact a result of complex layering techniques. The surface is applied as a painter would approach a canvas.

CLAY BODY
Low-fire white casting slip.

GLAZE
Selvin Clear: frit (3134) 41%, lithium carbonate 8%, china clay 25%, silica 27%.

FIRING
Electric kiln, cone 06 to 04 (1830°F to 1940°F/999°C to 1060°C) oxidation.

Nancy Selvin, *Rice Bowls,* cone 04 cast earthenware bowls, 3" x 4" x 3". Photo by Charles Frizzell.

MARC LEUTHOLD

UNITED STATES

I usually throw disks and then carve my textures with an X-acto knife and manipulate the form while it's still leather hard. Most of my sculptures stand on some kind of base after they are fired.

Glaze decisions are really hard for me. Probably like everyone else, I try to visualize what the piece will look like with various glazes. I do this while working on my sculptures. Since most of my work is not functional anymore, my glaze decisions are just visual. You might think almost any glaze or color would work on my forms, but I have to find just the right combinations. It takes time. I make tests, too.

Many of the sculptures are highly textured, like this one, so I do have to consider what sort of details may disappear underneath a glaze. I like lots of variations, and I like the glaze to break differently over edges and where it has variable thickness. I want the glaze to define the form. I don't want the viewer to see the form through a translucent glaze.

This Purple Matt glaze is chalky and light blue if applied thin. I like it thicker, when it becomes more intense in color. I use thick and thin applications to define the form. Glazes high in barium tend to give unusual variations; that's why we like them.

CLAY BODY

Red earthenware: Redart 65%, Goldart 15%, AP Green fireclay 10%, talc 10%. Add 1% fine grog.

GLAZE

Purple Matt: barium carbonate 43%, lithium carbonate 5%, nepheline syenite 20%, china clay 20%, silica 11%. Add 7% copper carbonate.

FIRING

Electric kiln, cone 04 (1940°F/1060°C) oxidation.

Marc Leuthold,
Purple Wheel, 2000,
cone 04 red earthenware,
6" diameter.
Photo by Eva Heyd.

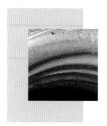

VINEET KACKER

INDIA

The imagery of this bottle comes from thoughts on the cosmic void and the dance of creation. There is a fair bit of movement in the piece, both in its body and in the traditional dancing figure on top. I wanted to use a simple matt glaze that would draw the eye in and let it travel about. This mustard-colored glaze seems to fit.

To further enhance the movement I used washes of iron oxide below the glaze and rutile above the glaze. These seem to allow the wood ash in the firing an opportunity to subtly color the surface of the sculpture. The rutile wash makes the flashing brighter, and both washes bring out the texture, shading the basic color of the glaze.

The piece is handbuilt and wheel thrown, although throwing a big doughnut is difficult. I am an architect, and I use clay and glaze to help me keep freedom in both arts. I also paint, and I like to use washes in clay work to add depth and to highlight throwing marks and hand textures as well as the movement in the form.

I fire rather fast with wood as the fuel instead of gas, and I know that even with a fast fire — about ten hours — I get some patina from the ash.

CLAY BODY

Earthenware: china clay 37.5%, ball clay 25%, fireclay 12.5%, feldspar 10%, silica 15%. Add 8% grog and 5% sand.

GLAZE

Greenish Satin Matt: potash feldspar 34%, whiting 21%, talc 3%, china clay 30%, silica 12%. Add 8% nickel oxide and 2% silicon carbide.

FIRING

Olsen-type fast-fire wood kiln, cone 04 (1940°F/1060°C).

Vineet Kacker, *Universe Bottle,* 2000, cone 04 earthenware, 23" x 15¹/₂" x 3¹/₂".
Photo by Anup Sood.

ANNABETH ROSEN

UNITED STATES

I build these pieces from very soft clay, very thick, and dry them for about a month. I do many glaze tests, always looking for interesting colors, modifying copper and cobalt, for instance, with iron chromate, iron oxide or nickel for more subtle hues. I vary coloring oxide percentages to get the variety I need for the intense color I want on the tiles. My glazing process has become more complicated to get richer color and depth. All of the work is multi-fired from cone 010 to as high as cone 3, with more glaze applications each time.

I prepare glazes as I go, in small batches of about 2000 grams, less than a gallon. This allows me to have a lot of color variations. Some of the colors come up very rich only from refiring and adding more glaze each time; the clay gets richer in color, too, from underneath. The white slip is applied to the raw dry tile first, then several glazes are applied for the first firing; sometimes I apply white slip again between layers of glaze for a textured quality. Usually there are three or four more firings. I stack the tiles on bits of broken shelves and lay a ring of silica powder underneath, to catch the molten glaze droplets from multiple firings.

Firing is extremely slow because the tiles are large and thicknesses vary up to several inches at least. I use a long pre-heat, about 50 degrees an hour to red heat (1300°F/704°C), often with a total 36-hour fire to cone 04 (1950°F/1066°C). Cooling must be slow too, about 100 to 150 degrees an hour to 1450°F (788°C) to keep the color intensity. After that, I cool 50 degrees an hour so that I don't shatter the thick pieces.

CLAY BODY

Red and white earthenware: ball clay and fireclay 80%, Custer feldspar 20%. Add 15% grog or silica sand.

ENGOBE

White slip: ball clay 25%, china clay 25%, Custer feldspar 25%, silica 25%.

GLAZE

Clear Gloss: frit (3403) 15%, frit (3417) 15%, frit (3626) 15%, Gerstley borate 35%, china clay 10%, silica 10%.

Variations

Yellow: add 2 to 8% red iron oxide.

Green: add 2 to 6% black copper oxide.

Purple: add 2 to 4% cobalt carbonate and 2 to 4% manganese dioxide.

Blue: add 2 to 3% cobalt carbonate.

FIRING

Electric kiln and gas kiln, cone 04 (1940°F/1060°C) oxidation.

Continued on page 42

Annabeth Rosen,
*Amber Oval with
Green Leaves,* 1996,
cone 04 enamel glazed tile,
$19^1/_2$" x 21" x 6".
Photo by Lee Fatherree.

Annabeth Rosen, *Birds with Blue Enamel* (detail), 1997, cone 04 enamel glazed tile, 19" x 20¹/₄" x 7¹/₂".
Photo by Lee Fatherree.

It took me years to realize how glaze can reveal nuances of the hand and amplify subtleties of ideas, and that the function of glaze is to manipulate and construct form with light and color. The elusive and ever-changing aspects of ceramics become increasingly beguiling as I continue to work.

Each piece, propelled by the prior one, must be a reinvention. I have a tendency to work very fast. I love the contrast of the beautiful glaze on the blunt shapes. I'm drawing and building the shapes with color. There is nothing else in the universe like clay and glaze.

I enjoy the results of fritted lead glazes, which are susceptible to minute changes in the kiln during firing and cooling. Different shapes glazed the same on the same piece may look different due to many variables. I search for a kind of understanding of my materials in order to know how to come close to what I dream of making. Once I come closer to this control,

I have to set up another goal, a different set of circumstances, so that the work can evolve. My interest is in how my ideas penetrate the material.

I break almost as much ceramics as I make, and I think I learn as much about the work by doing so. Being so focused on a destination for the piece, I overlook things, shapes, ideas. I get to see those in the broken parts. Much of my work is made from broken fired parts reassembled and reglazed, refired with the addition of new clay elements if necessary. I work with a hammer and chisel, and I think of the fired work as being as fluid and malleable as wet clay and glaze. Sometimes a broken shard is a more potent idea of the object than the object itself.

It can be more exciting to see one tile and imagine it in repetition than to actually see it repeated. My thinking is to have pattern where no pattern was intended, and rhythmic organization not by repetition but by accumulation.

MEDIUM FIRE

Sandra Black

Lynn Goodman

Linda Speranza

Tom Coleman

Anne Fallis Elliot

Bernardo Hogan

Pippin Drysdale

Victoria Shaw

Barbara Sorenson

Jeanne Otis

Virginia Scotchie

SANDRA BLACK

AUSTRALIA

I love this yellow color, and find that I can get it best by using glaze stains under a clear glaze. The Blythe's Golden Yellow stain I previously used has changed to a more orange-yellow. Now I make combination line blends with several yellow stains in 1% increments and test them under a clear glaze to get the yellow I want. Of course, these are tin-vanadium stains, and the Blythe colors are the most intense I have tested.

I blend the stains about half-and-half with porcelain slip, thin it with water, and airbrush it onto dry porcelain, then bisque fire. Before glazing I dip the pot in water — areas that are not sufficiently coated with the yellow mixture will show up and can be resprayed. Brushing the color on leaves streaks, so for a smooth surface, the color must be sprayed on. Too much moisture on the pot at once in spraying will cause air bubbles; take off the color and start over. If the coating is sufficient, apply the clear glaze and fire to cone 6.

With a passion for ceramics that are monochromatic, and a love of Fiesta ware, I have been testing colors for years. I find that the best, purest, most intense color comes in the above manner rather than by adding color to the glaze. This yellow color has a particular warmth and appeal for me; I use it a lot, but the technique works with any color.

It is true that the glaze must be applied evenly to get the even-all-over effect that I crave. If a clear glaze is too thick it gets cloudy, and if it is too thin the finished surface will vary or not seem to be glazed. I had to experiment a long time to gain the experience necessary for the right results from my methods of applying both the yellow color and the clear glaze over. I kept a lot of notes about my process and tried to measure raw glaze thickness by scratching through the glaze to measure the cross-section and to "feel" the thickness.

CLAY BODY
David Leach porcelain.

GLAZE
Any clear cone 6 glaze.

ENGOBE
Yellow: commercial yellow stains combined with porcelain slip.

FIRING
Electric kiln, cone 6 (2232°F/1222°C).

Sandra Black, untitled porcelain bowls. Photo by Victor France.

LYNNE GOODMAN

UNITED STATES

All my pieces are carved, then bisqued, then glazed using a latex-resist inlay method. I paint liquid latex on thick (thin latex is hard to remove) into all the carved areas and other places I want to mask off. When latex dries, it turns transparent yellow, then engobe or glaze can be brushed or sprayed over. Wash the brush with soap and water frequently, as latex will dry permanently and damage brushes.

I paint the background glaze color first using four to seven layers. Glaze should not be mixed too thick; it is better to apply many relatively thin layers of milk-consistency glaze for a really even coating. Wipe the latex design free of glaze before pulling off the resist material.

For the inlaid design I apply water-soluble wax resist over the glaze and draw designs through the wax that can be inlaid with other colored glazes. I chose this decorating technique because it is the best way to get the results I want, even though it is nitpicky and time-consuming. Actually, I do enjoy the process. It gives me crisp areas of color and depth from multiple layers of application.

I fire to cone 6 in approximately eight hours. I chose these glazes for my current work because they are well behaved, take stains easily for color, are compatible with other glazes, and give me the opportunity for matt or shiny finishes.

CLAY BODY
Commercial cone 6 porcelain.

GLAZES
DB2 Transparent: soda feldspar 45%, frit (3195) 13%, dolomite 6%, whiting 12%, china clay 2%, silica 21%. Add 5% various Mason stains.

Satin: Custer feldspar 64%, talc 5%, whiting 18%, china clay 9%, silica 5%. Add 5% various Mason stains (particularly good for chrome-tin pinks).

FIRING
Electric kiln, cone 6 (2232°F/1222°C).

Lynn Goodman, untitled plate, cone 6 porcelain, carved and inlaid, with gold luster, 13" x 3".
Photo by Lynn Goodman.

LINDA SPERANZA

UNITED STATES

My platters are made of heavily grogged clay, covered leather hard with three coats of Shino slip. The platters are about 30 inches wide by ⁵/₈ inch thick, with a foot 2¹/₂ inches high by ¹/₂ inch thick. They require about 40 pounds of clay. They are pressed over a round plaster hump mold, paddled and articulated.

I would like the viewer to look down through layers of color, feeling depth. I formulate glazes to create an interplay where they overlap for a rich illusion of depth. If the glazing doesn't satisfy me, I apply more glaze and fire again. Over the top of the glaze I poured an X of Shino slip. I rarely repeat the same combinations; exploration is the most fun.

I apply layers of glaze in many coats. Since raw liquid glazes mostly look alike, I have to retain a mental vision of what I've done, overlapping and crossing coats, creating textures. Some of my glazes are soft and flaky on the surface, but I don't add any hardener to the glaze, so they will be sure to crawl. My glazes need to be applied in rapid succession, just barely waiting for the previous one to dry. If you wait too long the glazes may not bond.

I impress spirals in the clay to symbolize the journey through the ebbs and flows of life.

CLAY BODY
Mixture of two commercial white and red stoneware clays.

GLAZES
Base: barium carbonate 50%, nepheline syenite 50%.

Variation #1
Saturated Blue: 5% copper carbonate.

Variation #2
Gray-Yellow: 10% rutile.

Green Snakeskin: barium carbonate 30%, nepheline syenite 50%, magnesium carbonate 20%. Add 5% copper carbonate.

Lavender Matt: nepheline syenite 30%, flint 15%, dolomite 15%, magnesium carbonate 15%, spodumene 10%, barium carbonate 10%, china clay 5%. Add 5% cobalt carbonate.

SLIP
Shino slip: nepheline syenite 38%, soda spar 9%, spodumene 13%, soda ash 3%, china clay 24%, ball clay 13%.

FIRING
Gas kiln, cone 6 (2232°F/1222°C) reduction.

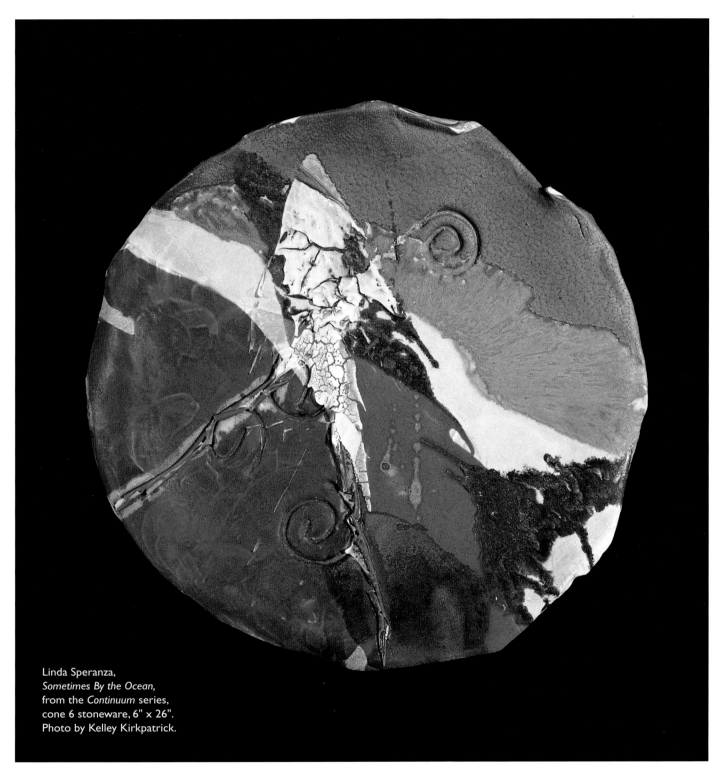

Linda Speranza,
Sometimes By the Ocean,
from the *Continuum* series,
cone 6 stoneware, 6" x 26".
Photo by Kelley Kirkpatrick.

TOM COLEMAN
UNITED STATES

The teapot was constructed using slab pieces thrown over bisqued hump molds, regular wheel-thrown shapes, and press-molded pieces. Then I apply a slip made from the same clay body, plus 10% Cerdec (Degussa in Europe) Orange Stain 23616, to the leather-hard parts where I want orange. The pot is fired to cone 6 in a gas kiln, oxidation, for a vitreous body.

After bisque, the orange parts are brushed with liquid latex resist. Then I spray on the Bright Blue glaze, pull off the latex, and fire again to cone 04. Finally the piece is coated with the Textural Slip glaze, which is meant to crack, sprayed very thick over. After the slip dries some pieces might curl or start to fall off. To make sure the remaining loose pieces don't fall off on your kiln shelf, take an air nozzle and gently blow them off. After the last firing is completed, to cone 06, you should have a mud-cracked surface with the brilliant colored underglaze exposed.

My inspiration is the Las Vegas desert and the bright colored neon of downtown against the dry, cracked, textured earth.

CLAY BODY
Commercial white clay.

GLAZES
Bright Blue: barium carbonate 42%, lithium carbonate 7%, nepheline syenite 21%, china clay 21%, silica 11%. Add 6% copper oxide.

Textural slip glaze: Gerstley borate 46%, borax 4%, magnesium carbonate 31%, china clay 19%.

FIRING
Bisque to cone 6 (2232°F/1222°C), glaze fire to cone 04 (1940°F/1060°C) and cone 06 (1830°F/999°C).

Tom Coleman,
Cobalt Treatment,
cone 6 stoneware teapot,
26"x 24" x 3".
Photo by O'Gara Photography.

ANNE FALLIS ELLIOT

UNITED STATES

This glaze varies according to the wood ash used. Some woods, washed and unwashed, are more refractory than others, so keep track. I mix the batch by weight, fill a five-gallon pail half full of water and add the dry glaze material. The mixture sits for 24 hours, then the liquid batch is sieved through a window screen. If the glaze is lumpy I screen it again. The glaze should cover a finger so that the skin does not show through, but not too thick and not too thin.

I dip the bisque pots once in this mixture and dry them overnight, then fire to cone 6 in the electric kiln. Ashes are impure and can create bubbles during the firing, which I don't mind. These are more sculptures than functional pots.

I throw all the watering cans, lidded jars and teapots that I make. But I throw the bottoms, tops and lids separately and flat like a flat plate, then throw the middle section and spouts, and pull the handles. I usually leave the finger marks. The middle parts, thrown without top and bottom, are immediately altered to irregular oval shapes. All parts are assembled, beginning from and fitted to the middle shape.

My forms have changed over the years, but I have never caught on to color. I've always loved black. Ash brings out texture and adds a surprise element.

CLAY BODY
Commercial smooth white stoneware.

GLAZE
Gunmetal Black Matt:
unwashed wood ash 25%, nepheline syenite 38%, talc 19%, ball clay 19%. Add 4% black copper oxide, 3% black cobalt oxide, 2.5% red iron oxide.

FIRING
Electric kiln, cone 6 (2232°F/1222°C).

Anne Fallis Elliot,
untitled, cone 6 white stoneware teapot
with black ash glaze, $9^{1}/_{2}$" x $8^{3}/_{4}$" x $5^{1}/_{2}$".
Photo by Kevin Noble.

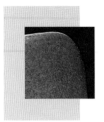

BERNARDO HOGAN

PUERTO RICO

This vase is wheel thrown, cut in half, reconstructed and converted into an oval. When it is leather hard I texture the surface with a natural sponge, using slip from the same body of clay as the vessel. The surface quality depends on how much sponged texture was applied on the raw clay. To obtain more texture I use different sizes of sponge. I sometimes add ceramic pigments to the slip I texture with. I bisque fire to cone 05.

Glaze is sprayed inside and out — in this case, Gray in and Tuscany Red, which is rather matt, out. After glazing I fire to cone 3 in an electric kiln.

I was always interested in geology and became interested in ceramics through learning about clays. In the process of preparing glazes for Susana Espinosa, a ceramist, I came to understand the technical aspect of the raw materials in ceramics.

The creative process involves the reconstruction of the pottery vase by flattening or displacing the piece. Preparing a glaze and applying it to a particular form is a process I enjoy because it encompasses the capability of the particular glaze batch to sustain the reconstruction of the original form.

CLAY BODY
Goldart 40%, fireclay 18%, soda feldspar 15%, china clay 12%, grog 15%.

GLAZES
Gray: frit (3134) 9.5%, spodumene 35, talc 34%, china clay 20.5%. Add 0.2% cobalt carbonate and 3% rutile.

Tuscany Red: barium carbonate 45%, frit (3134) 15%, calcined zinc 13.5%, china clay 16.5%, silica 10%. Add 2% green nickel carbonate.

FIRING
Electric kiln, cone 3 (2134°F/1168°C).

54

Bernardo Hogan, *Tuscany Red,* cone 3 vessel, 18¹/₂" x 10". Photo by John Betancourt.

PIPPIN DRYSDALE

AUSTRALIA

Mixing stains and developing the colors I want is a matter of experimenting. I make so many different colors and use most of the stains in a very concentrated amount of 20% — more than usual for glaze colorants.

The Karakorum influence is very strong. This small region of Pakistan, and the major truck route that passes through it, are of vital importance to the economic and human needs of northern Pakistan. The variety of produce, particularly the fruits, impressed me because their colors are my colors.

I spray the barium glaze on bisque and then do a series of four or five waxing layers, between which I incise marks that I inlay with different colored glazes. The high amount of barium in this glaze induces fabulous colors with stains and oxides. I use all the glaze techniques: pouring, dipping, brushing, spraying, resist, incising, inlaying and layering.

Due to the amount of wax on the pots, it is necessary to leave the lid of the kiln open about an inch, and the plugs out, for the first two hours on the low setting. I can remove the lid if necessary, even when the elements have been turned to medium or high, to be rid of the smoke. The wax is usually gone when I turn the switches to high. Because of the layers of glaze application, I use a thick wash of 40% china clay and 60% alumina hydrate or calcined alumina to protect the shelves from glaze droppings.

My main concerns are with color. I love color! I'm passionate about it. I spend a great deal of time testing and developing variations with glaze stains and oxides.

There is also the surprise and joy of the glazes fusing together due to the thick applications. This creates gems! So often colors come and go, never to be seen again, but if you don't take risks with extreme amounts, these effects can't be achieved. Commitment, that's all I have to say.

CLAY BODY
Cone 6 porcelain.

GLAZE
Barium carbonate 15.5%, frit (4113 or 3124) 19%, magnesite 8%, potash feldspar 47%, whiting 8%, ball clay 3%. Add about 20% Blythe and Degussa stains.

FIRING
Electric kiln, cone 6 (2232°F/1222°C).

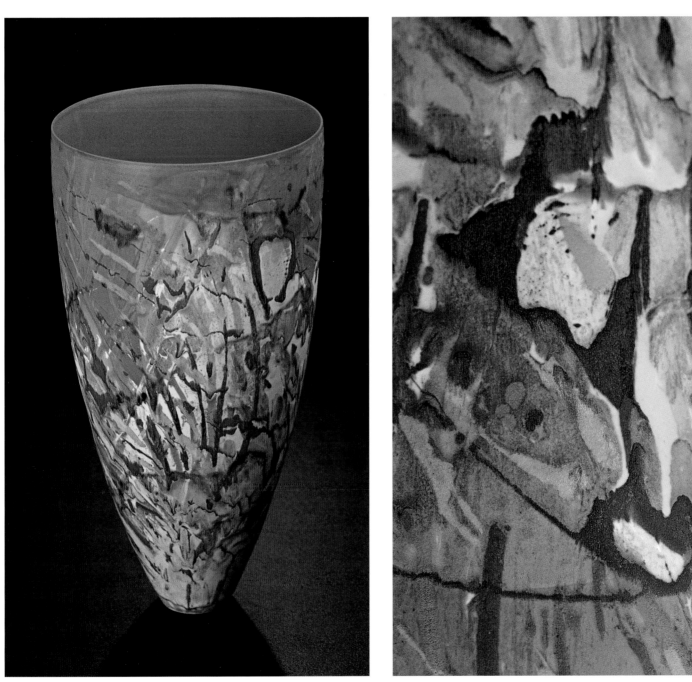

Pippin Drysdale, *Karakorum Bounty,* 2000, from the *Pakistan* series, cone 6 porcelain vessel, 19" high. Photo by Robert Frith.

VICTORIA SHAW

UNITED STATES

This totem is fabricated from an extruder, in sections cut with a wire at various angles. The angles are capped with clay slabs, and I use a rasp to give a rough surface. I cut a $^3/_4$-inch hole through the top and bottom of each piece so that it can accommodate a plumbing pipe for installation.

I spray the glaze on the bisqued pieces with an airbrush. Each piece is fired individually on stilts so that the glaze surrounds the form entirely. I make more forms than needed and play with the structure when I assemble them on the pipe. I test lots of glazes and use many different ones on my sculptures. Iris Blue was chosen for its silky matt surface and the deep blue and purple highlights. This glaze also produces crystal formations on the surface, which is a natural reinforcement of the hexagonal shapes in the sculpture.

If the glaze is on an iron-bearing body you will get dark edges under the blue. The application needs to be of medium thickness; take care to avoid thick spots, or it will become muddy and shiny. Zinc enhances the blue. I might modify it with manganese and strontium to make it more purple.

CLAY BODY
Commercial sculpture stoneware.

GLAZE
Iris Blue: soda feldspar 53%, whiting 16%, calcined zinc 12%, china clay 14%, silica 5%.

Variations
Light Blue: add 1.5% cobalt carbonate.

Darker Blue (as seen on *Ancestral Icon*): add 2.5% cobalt carbonate.

FIRING
Electric kiln, cone 6 (2232°F/1222°C) oxidation.

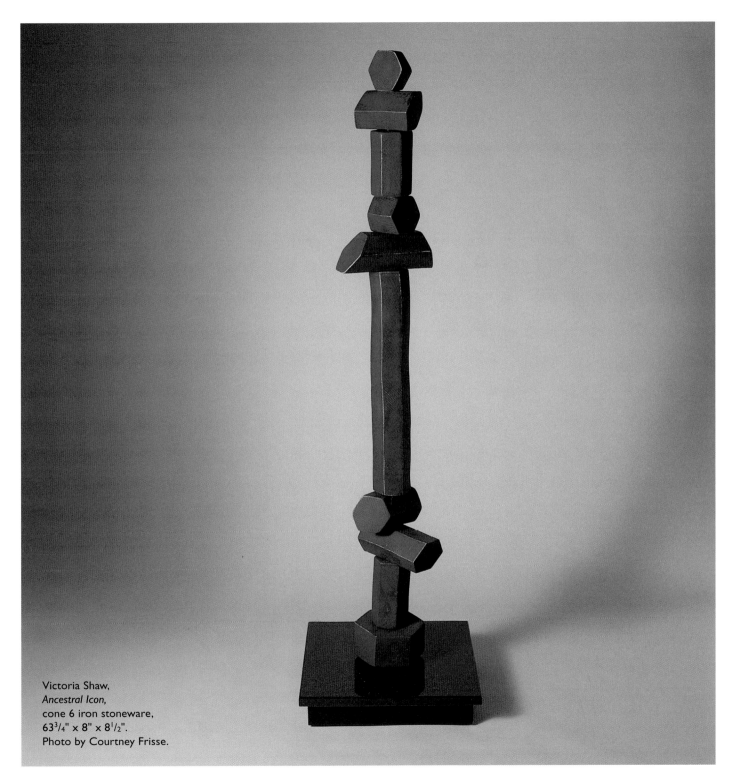

Victoria Shaw,
Ancestral Icon,
cone 6 iron stoneware,
63³/₄" x 8" x 8¹/₂".
Photo by Courtney Frisse.

BARBARA SORENSON

UNITED STATES

I use a combination of vitreous engobes and flashing slips to react with the final throw of soda into the kiln and give me the quality of the strata of the earth's crust. Paper clay allows great manipulation in handbuilding methods. I add impurities and grog to give the fired sculpture a texture like dirt, and saturate the slips and engobes with colorants to achieve maximum intensity. The interiors are brushed with the manganese glaze on greenware. On the outside, engobes are applied, and the pot is once-fired upside down in a gas kiln to cone 6 in reduction.

When the cone is down I spray a mix of approximately four pounds of baking soda to three gallons of boiling water into the kiln with 60 pounds pressure on the air compressor. The flashing slips react dramatically with the soda and the colored engobes. The soda brightens the colors and flashes the slips, bringing out the natural orange of china clay.

To me, the effect seems to mimic the metamorphic process of the evolution of the earth. The soda deposits on all the surfaces, adding a unified softness to the color palette.

CLAY BODY

Commercial paper clay with grog.

GLAZE

Manganese Matt: nepheline syenite 64%, spodumene 9%, lithium carbonate 4%, soda ash 4%, ball clay 19%. Add 3% manganese dioxide, 3% red iron oxide, 0.3% cobalt carbonate.

FLASHING SLIPS

Helmer's: Helmer kaolin 100%. Add 20% bentonite.

Bauer Orange: china clay 45%, ball clay 40%, borax 5%, Zircopax 10%.

VITREOUS ENGOBES

First engobe: Gerstley borate 25%, china clay 25%, ball clay 25%, silica 25%. Add 15 to 20% stains.

Second engobe: nepheline syenite 14%, china clay 43%, ball clay 43%. Add 15 to 20% stains.

FIRING

Gas kiln, cone 6 (2232°F/1222°C) in reduction.

Barbara Sorensen, *Three Graces,* 1999, cone 6 stoneware and stones, 45" x 19" x 16". Photo by Brad Miller.

JEANNE OTIS
UNITED STATES

I began my career in ceramics with a degree in painting, where my interest lay in color field abstracts. I previously made large asymmetrical wall pieces. Now I am interested in small-scale tiles in installations that hold at a distance as well as close, like a photograph does. The use of the crawling glaze adds a surprise element to close-up viewing.

I manipulate the Giraffe Pattern glaze to make the final pattern go from small to very large chunks. I can go from a dry-brush look to a textured, 3-D, broken look. I like the matt, chunky thick glaze against the matt clay surface, and working intuitively, I color the clay with combinations of stains and frits. For the black color I use 70% black stain mixed with 30% frit. For the warm gray I use 80% stain — warm and cool grays combined — mixed with 20% Ferro frit 3124. The soft gray-blue color is Mason stain 6540 in a vitreous engobe.

Everything is fired and refired three to five times in an electric kiln I designed for flat slabs. It is a large box, long and wide but not very high: 54" by 33" by 18". The lid is counter-balanced, and there is a second door at one end to slide slabs into it instead of lifting them. The firing takes 20 hours.

CLAY BODY
White stoneware.

GLAZE
Giraffe Pattern Crawl: magnesium carbonate 31%, soda feldspar 31%, frit (3134) 6.2%, whiting 7.4%, zinc oxide 5.7%, china clay 18.7%.

FIRING
Electric kiln, cone 5 (2185°F/1196°C), multiple firings.

Jeanne Otis, *Tempest Portal,* 1999, cone 5 stoneware, 25$^{1}/_{2}$" x 18" x 1". Photos by Jeanne Otis.

VIRGINIA SCOTCHIE

UNITED STATES

I use a coil-slab process and pinch the forms, then stretch them with a wooden paddle. Some parts of the forms come from plaster press molds or wooden dowels wrapped in newspaper with clay slabs wrapped around. These could be tiny objects, but they are larger than they look in the photographs.

The two very different glazes juxtapose or sometimes divide a piece in half. The bronze metallic emphasizes a human-made tool, and the crawl glaze, which was originally given to me by Adriana Baler, relates to nature and the earth: earth/tool, man/nature, mechanical/natural.

After bisque firing at cone 04, I fire the bronze luster glaze on at cone 2 to harden it. That way, I can easily wipe off any crawl glaze that abuts it. I apply the crawl glaze next, then fire to cone 6 in the electric kiln. I mix the crawl glaze thick and don't sieve, applying it in layers with a sponge, like stucco. Often I repeat the process and refire as many as three more times to build up the craggy surface and add depth of color.

CLAY BODY
AP Green fireclay 20%, Hawthorne fireclay 15%, local red clay 15%, kyanite 20%, ball clay 20%, fine grog 5%, medium grog 5%.

GLAZES
Bronze: Redart clay 60%, Gerstley borate 30%, ball clay 5%, silica 5%. Add 45% manganese dioxide, 5% copper carbonate, 5% cobalt oxide.

Base Crawl: bone ash 77%, cryolite 14%, soda feldspar 8.6%, barium carbonate 0.4%.

Variations
Pink (shown): add 14% Mason stain 6121.

Turquoise (shown): add 4% copper carbonate.

Yellow-Orange (shown): add 13% Mason stain 6471.

Indigo (shown): add 3% cobalt oxide.

Orange: add 8% rutile.

Purple: add 3% cobalt oxide.

Green: add 2% chrome oxide.

Avocado green: add 14% Mason stain 6280.

FIRING
Electric kiln, cone 6 (2232°F/1222°C) oxidation.

Continued on page 66

Virginia Scotchie, *Bronze Spout/Pink Cup,* 2000, cone 6 stoneware, 8" x 7" x 18". Photo by Brian Dressler.

Virginia Scotchie, *Yellow Sieve/Bronze Handle,* 1999, cone 6 stoneware, 12" x 12" x 21". Photos by Brian Dressler.

Indigo/Bronze Spout, 2000, cone 6 stoneware, 8" x 7" x 18".

Turquoise Funnel, 2000, cone 6 stoneware, 7" x 11" x 20".

HIGH FIRE

Hwang Jeng-Daw

Hein Severijns

Val Cushing

Maria Ana Gutierrez

Gillian Hodge

Tapio Yli-Viikari

Cathi Jefferson

Jeroen Bechtold

Maria Bofill

Piet Stockmans

Fritz Rossman

Robert Pulley

Ray Meeker

Bai Ming

Greg Daly

Sequoia Miller

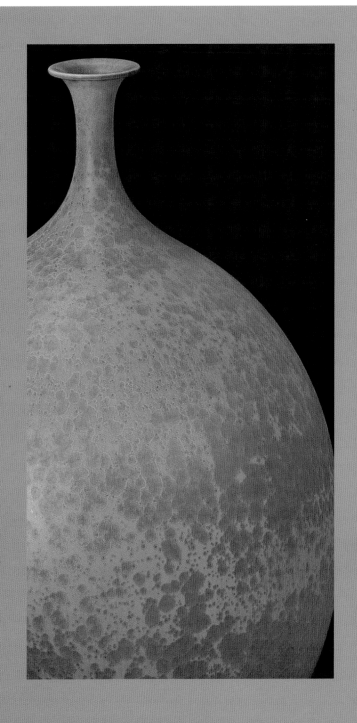

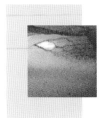

HWANG JENG-DAW

CHINA

This teapot is thrown, with a coil-built handle and a handbuilt spout. The style is derived from a traditional Chinese YiXing teapot. For me, that style is too Chinese and too rigid, so being a modern teapot maker, I tried to design it with more beautifully curved lines. I use the purple and blue glazes to express the most elegant and royal colors — in my mind, at least — not the symbolic Chinese royal colors like yellow and gold.

I think that Taiwan ball clay is similar to Kentucky ball clay, rather dark. There is no real substitute for YiXing clay from Taiwan or from China, but any fine-grained red earthenware could work. I am sorry, but I do not know anyone who is marketing YiXing clay in the rest of the world. I dip the purple glaze first on the bisqued pot, then spray the light blue glaze over that. Firing is in oxidation in an electric kiln.

I live in Taiwan but I stay about two months in China and two months in the United States every year. Most of my works are teapots. I drink tea and enjoy the making of all kinds of teapots. For me they are very good glaze experiments.

CLAY BODY
Taiwan ball clay 85%, Chinese YiXing clay 5%, extra fine grog 9%, red iron oxide 1%.

GLAZES
Purple: potash feldspar 40%, talc 17%, whiting 9%, barium carbonate 8%, dolomite 5%, zinc oxide 5%, silica 16%. Add 15% zirconium silicate, 3% cobalt oxide, 2% manganese dioxide.

Light Blue: soda feldspar 73%, whiting 8%, magnesium carbonate 6%, zinc oxide 5%, ball clay 3%, silica 5%. Add 5% copper oxide.

FIRING
Electric kiln, cone 8 (2305°F/1263°C) oxidation.

Hwang Jeng-Daw, *Righteous Teapot,* cone 8 stoneware, 10" x 7" x 14". Photo by Cheng Fui-yun.

HEIN SEVERIJNS

THE NETHERLANDS

make only thrown forms, especially classically shaped bottles in porcelain, and use only my own crystalline glazes developed over many years. I search for a harmony between form and glaze when applying my satin matt crystallines. For an agreeable touch I polish the glazed surface after firing with a very fine carborundum paper.

Matt crystalline glazes are very difficult to control, more so than glossy ones I think, but they are astonishingly fun. My glaze is applied in layers, as follows. First layer, spray on the tin and titanium mix, normal thickness. For blue, spray on next the cobalt mixture, thin. For green, spray on next the copper mixture, thin. Over each colored layer, spray the iron mixture, thin. You can add additional layers of nickel, manganese or vanadium. Finish all with a thin layer of the base recipe, then with a mix of the base plus 2% molybdenum oxide. I use up to seven layers.

I fire as fast as possible to cone 10 (2340°F/1280°C) and cool to cone 02, (2014°F/1100°C) for seeding crystals. Then I go back up to 2100°F (1150°C) — about cone 3 — hold there for three hours, and then cool with steps of 20 degrees each half hour to 1880°F (1000°C), about cone 05. At this point, I shut off the kiln. Firing for crystals is very tricky, and you may have to practice and change schedules a little at a time.

CLAY BODY
Limoges porcelain.

GLAZE
Crystalline Satin Matt: potash feldspar 32%, soda feldspar 12%, barium carbonate 18%, zinc oxide 15%, lead bisilicate 5%, talc 5%, whiting 3%, china clay 5%, silica 5%.

Variations
Opaque: add 5% tin oxide, 5% titanium dioxide.

Blue: add 2% cobalt oxide.

Green: add 4% copper carbonate.

Brown: add 8% red iron oxide.

FIRING
Electric kiln, cone 10 (2381°F/1305°C) oxidation, special cooling.

Hein Severijns,
Spherical Pot with Crystalline Glaze,
cone 10 porcelain, 16$\frac{1}{2}$".

VAL CUSHING

UNITED STATES

The idea for this piece and others like it comes from the architectural column. This piece is wheel thrown, thick walled and solid looking. The warm, velvety semi-matt glaze — the color of ripe persimmon — invites the touch and brings you closer to it, the way a smooth marble surface or an ocean-tossed stone does.

The pot is dipped in the glaze; the lid and faceted lower section have a wash of iron oxide on the bisque under the glaze. Firing in the gas kiln in reduction atmosphere is crucial to produce the rich, warm, persimmon color. Here is the cycle:

1) Oxidation up to cone 010.
2) Begin reduction cone 010, forcing 10 to 12 inches of flame out spy holes for one hour.
3) Begin partial reduction by opening damper slightly, giving a shorter back-pressure flame, 6 to 8 inches.
4) Partial reduction continues eight hours, the last two hours from cone 8 to cone 10 half over.
5) When cone 10 is half over, oxidize 15 minutes by pulling out the damper so there is no back-pressure flame.
6) Turn off gas, close kiln completely everywhere; cool slowly so that oxidation brings iron effects to reds and oranges. The kiln is cooled for 36 hours before being opened.

CLAY BODY

Stoneware: Goldart 40%, AP Green fireclay 24%, ball clay 12%, Barnard clay 4%, soda feldspar 10%, silica 4%, fine grog 6%.

GLAZES

Mixture of *Mamo Matt* (40%) and *Shaner's Red* (60%).

Mamo Matt: potash feldspar 25%, soda feldspar 25%, dolomite 20%, whiting 5%, china clay 10%, calcined china clay 15%. Add 4% tin oxide.

Shaner's Red: Custer potash feldspar 52%, whiting 21%, talc 4%, china clay 7%, calcined china clay 16%. Add 4% bone ash, 4% red iron oxide.

FIRING

Gas kiln, cone 10 (2381°F/1305°C) reduction.

Val Cushing, covered jar from the *Column* series, cone 10 stoneware, 34" x 8".

MARIA ANA GUTIERREZ

UNITED STATES

The surfaces on my cylinders are like canvases. I chose the cylinder as a base due to its simplicity and elegance and the opportunity for multiple views and moods. I don't want the piece to have a front and a back, but a series of possibilities like the serpent biting its tail. Because the shape is so vertical I work with several layers. On each piece I generally work with a variety of glazes chosen from about 40 types.

First I sprayed this cylinder with So Shino, then brushed Ruth's Green horizontally, and over that Bray Shino. I scratched the glaze, exposing the clay, and inlaid Tomato Red. I finished the composition with Black Slip Trail lines across the design. The degree of reduction is responsible for the orange color and the spots. I hold the reduction at the end of the cone 10 firing in the gas kiln.

I glaze the inside of my pieces with a color that either complements or contrasts with the exterior surface. I'm interested in glazes that have a good effect when used thinly, layer on layer. I paint, brush, spray, sponge, slip-trail and use any other method I can think of. I'm also looking for glazes that interact well with a base glaze to add color, texture, bubbles, blisters and sheen, make it matt and so forth. I have hundreds of tests with glaze combinations, and I am constantly testing new ones.

CLAY BODY
Heavy iron stoneware.

GLAZES
So Shino: nepheline syenite 65%, table salt 4.5% (dissolve in boiling water), ball clay 13%, china clay 8%, Redart clay 4.5%, tin oxide 5%.

Bray Shino: nepheline syenite 45%, soda feldspar 19%, spodumene 15%, soda ash 4%, ball clay 17%.

Ruth's Green: potash feldspar 40%, whiting 21%, china clay 39%. Add 4% copper oxide.

Tomato Red: soda feldspar 45%, bone ash 10.7%, magnesium carbonate 6.7%, china clay 6.7%, silica 24.2%, red iron oxide 6.7%.

Black Slip Trail: soda feldspar 80%, barium carbonate 10%, china clay 10%. Add 10% Mason black stain.

FIRING
Gas kiln, cone 10 (2381°F/1305°C) reduction.

Maria Ana Gutierrez, untitled cylinder, cone 10 porcelain, 4" x 4" x 11".

GILLIAN HODGE

UNITED STATES

Maen is an old Cornish name for a cliff fortification; somehow it seemed to reflect the woman who must be open to experience and yet strong and contained, a dilemma that seemed to confront this piece. The glazes are as important as the form. They need to reflect the voice of the work, the inner meaning as far as I know it. Natural glazes seem to me to bear their matrix with them, their rocky antecedents, but I also wanted some idea of the ocean seen from a cliff, a dull blue that the ash develops from cobalt wash.

I build with coils and slabs, with inner structures. I have drawings of the piece, but generally the work changes. I thin the clay as I go, beating it against my hand with wooden paddles from the beach in various sizes. The finished sculpture looks heavy but is remarkably light. I dry it slowly under plastic.

The base of this piece is brushed with a wash of red iron oxide and table salt, for a rich red. My washes are oxide and water mixed by eye, with experience. I use cheap hardware-store brushes. I fire raw, so I use a light touch with the glaze; natural glazes tend to vary in application, but the underlying body reacts well to that. The chief problem with ash-clay mixtures is to see where they have gone on as they are slurped up by the dry clay. I incise a line lightly in the clay where I begin. Sometimes I rub the dry glaze into the dry clay. The trouble with all this is that experience counts, as does a long knowledge of materials and a well-known kiln.

Firing to cone 10 takes two days. I make constant adjustments by changing the orifices on the burners throughout the fire, a really difficult task. Reduction begins at cone 03. The kiln takes three days to cool.

CLAY BODY
Commercial stoneware plus scrap.

ENGOBE
Prospected clay from Okanagan Valley, British Columbia.

GLAZES
Wild glaze #1: prospected clay from Tyler Foote, Nevada City 80%, Custer potash feldspar 20%.

Wild glaze #2: oak ash 80%, any feldspar 20%.

FIRING
Gas or wood-fire kiln, cone 10 (2381°F/1305°C) reduction.

Gillian Hodge, *Maen,* 1999, cone 10 porcelain figure, once-fired, 24" x 12" x 30". Photos by Gene Crowe.

TAPIO YLI-VIIKARI

FINLAND

My idea about the shape was to make thrown platters plain and simple, to reduce the expression of the shape to the minimal and let the material and the glaze have the energy. I add 10% very fine molochite to the body to minimize shrinkage; it does not destroy the fineness.

I felt the glazing had to be simple too. I first painted a square with the temmoku glaze and then sprayed the piece all over with celadon. Both glazes are quite thick. The edge and the underside of the plate were finished with a wash of iron oxide and manganese dioxide; this is something I learned as a student, from Kyllikki Salmenhaara. She told me if you do not quite like the clay you are working with, you can help it by painting the dry clay just thinly with iron for firing at high temperature. This is a Swedish-Finnish thing to do; many of those clay artists used this technique on porcelain in the 1930s and 1940s.

Celadons and temmokus are international glazes. I have exchanged teaching positions in America, and these glazes may have come from Cranbrook. Who knows? We experiment from other beginnings!

CLAY BODY
Fine-grained white commercial stoneware.

GLAZES
Temmoku: potash feldspar 35%, whiting 30%, china clay 15%, silica 20%. Add 10% red iron oxide.

Celadon: potash feldspar 27%, whiting 20%, china clay 20%, silica 33%. Add 1% red iron oxide.

FIRING:
Gas kiln, cone 9 to 10 (2336°F to 2381°F/1280°C to 1305°C) reduction.

Tapio Yli-Viikari, *Timepiece,* cone 10 stoneware platter with celadon and temmoku glazes, 20" x 2". Photo by Timo Kauppila.

CATHI JEFFERSON
CANADA

The inspiration for this bowl is derived from native grass baskets. The pot is thrown upside down and then altered, and a bottom is attached. The design can be symbolic of many things — food, gathering, bounty. After bisque firing, the piece was dipped in Helmer Kaolin Wash, thin like skim milk. I don't let it drip because drips show.

Sometimes I pencil the design. The body of the wheat is applied with a sponge stamp dipped in rutile terra sigillata. I think of wheat moving and leaning in the wind. Then the stalks are brushed down from each head of wheat. Finally each strand of wheat is highlighted with the Brown Outline, using a fine brush. Last, the Shino is poured inside, as its warmth and tone will feel right against the salted exterior.

I begin firing around midnight with burners on low, until cone 08 in the morning, when light reduction begins. When cone 9 is down I start dropping in "burritos" made of road salt six parts, baking soda four parts, combined with dampened wood shavings and rolled in moistened newspaper. My 40-cubic-foot kiln requires three pounds of salt and one and one-half pounds of baking soda. This is all the salt/soda required to give results with a rich variety of texture and tone.

Pottery forms evolve as canvases. The squared sides symbolize a window or door frame, with nature seen through each frame, or a basic abstract design that's always trying to relate shape with design.

CLAY BODY
Commercial buff stoneware.

GLAZES
Helmer Kaolin wash: Helmer kaolin 80%, nepheline syenite 20%.

Mackenzie Shino: potash feldspar 42%, spodumene (with iron) 36%, soda ash 9%, china clay 12%.

TERRA SIGILLATA
4500 grams ball clay, 3 gallons water, 48 grams Calgon or lye. Let stand 24 hours, siphon and use the top two-thirds; discard the bottom third.

Variations
Rutile terra sigillata: add 20 grams rutile to 100 ml sigillata.

Brown Outline: add 5 tbsp Mason stain 6134 to 500 ml sigillata.

FIRING
Gas kiln, cone 10 (2381°F/ 1305°C) salt/soda reduction.

Cathi Jefferson, *Wheat Bowl*, cone 10 porcelaneous stoneware, salt/soda-fired, 24" x 12" x 14". Photo by John Sinal.

JEROEN BECHTOLD

THE NETHERLANDS

Glaze to me is like paint to a painter: it enhances what you want to express. Lusters and bright colors like blue shout for attention. The cast bowls in this case were so basic, they demanded a basic ceramic glaze. Cobalt blue, can you get more basic?

The feet are not glazed; they are cut to make sharp edges in contrast to the soft, glazed feeling of the bowl.

I make my own models and molds, except for the occasional shape I can use. Mostly I alter the casts that come from the molds. Casting is a boring technique, so the moment the clay is free of the mold I start altering. The advantage of cast clay over thrown clay is that the clay has no "direction." I also like the consistent wall thickness.

I experiment on the work right away, without making tests. All I do is try to foresee what might happen and live with the result, as it usually turns out to be better than what I imagine. When you allow ceramics to speak for itself it can give you so much.

Sometimes I use colored glazes — instead of clear — under lusters on the insides of my pieces, just to see what will happen. This piece has clear glaze under the three lusters. Firing is very fast in my electric kiln, about five hours to about cone 10. The lusters are painted on, and the piece is fired again to about cone 015. Actually, I don't use cones; I use the computer controller, which does a better job.

CLAY BODY
Limoges porcelain casting clay.

GLAZE
Clear Mottled: potash feldspar 50%, whiting 16.7%, talc 2.3%, lithium carbonate 1%, zinc oxide 1%, silica 29%.

Variation
Blue: add 12% cobalt carbonate.

LUSTERS
Commercial platinum, bronze and mother of pearl.

FIRING
Gas kiln, cone 10 (2381°F/ 1305°C) oxidation; luster: cone 017 (1377°F/747°C).

Jeroen Bechtold, *Sacred Trinity,* 1999, cone 10 porcelain, 35" x 35" x 13". Photo by Anita de Jong.

MARIA BOFILL

SPAIN

I repeat the old symbol of the labyrinth, where I introduce a world of perspective with a dialogue between the wall and the emptiness that this wall involves. Blue, white and gold are for me the most characteristic colors from the Mediterranean, the place where I live. My work tends to create objects without function, a search fluctuating between a classicist trend and a contemporary break. I like natural and living things that seem to be in motion. In that sense I consider my pieces small architectonic objects.

I work only with porcelain and normally have four firings: first I bisque at about cone 08 in the electric kiln in 14 to 16 hours. The second firing is to cone 10 or 11 in the gas kiln in reduction atmosphere with no glaze, to vitrify the porcelain. Then I spray the blue engobe and brush the transparent glaze and fire again to cone 10 in the electric kiln in oxidizing atmosphere. The fourth firing is to about cone 015. This is for the liquid gold, which is applied by brush.

Sometimes I add impurities to the clay body for a little texture. I work in a small studio, in a small space up flights of stairs. This may account for the small scale of my work, the thin sections, the convoluted shapes, which, I hope, have big ideas.

CLAY BODY
Limoges porcelain.

ENGOBE
Blue: cobalt blue stain 50%, porcelain body 30%, transparent frit 20%.

GLAZES
Clear: potash feldspar 80%, whiting 20%.

LUSTER
Gold: manufactured by Brendle (Barcelona).

FIRING
Gas and electric kilns, cone 10 (2381°F/1305°C) and 015 (1470°F/800°C).

Maria Bofill, untitled, from the *Labyrinth* series, cone 10 porcelain,
11" diameter x 2" (top) and 9" diameter x 4".

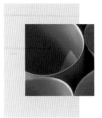

PIET STOCKMANS

BELGIUM

I chose this color, glaze and technique because I like it. The wash of cobalt is covered by dips of the glaze in certain areas and no glaze in certain areas. I am an industrial designer, but I also have my own studio and my own kiln. This group of vessels is installed in a wooden box.

Creation is the result of activity and not of thinking. It is activity that generates ideas, which themselves give rise to other ideas. It is a process in the course of which decisive choices are made in a mysterious way. It is the mechanism with which the farmer plows the fields, a phenomenon that can be compared to the way prayers are used, mantras recited, or everyday gestures repeated. It is a quest for simplicity, peace, physical well-being.

Porcelain is a material for art. It's as useful as acrylics, lapis lazuli or polyester, only it has to be looked at in new ways. One immediately associates porcelain with Chinese and Japanese figurines, or European porcelains, or nicely decorated dinner services. I felt it was urgent to break this traditional image and to show that in the material of porcelain and glaze, quite extraordinary things can be made and constructed.

CLAY BODY
Limoges porcelain, eggshell thin.

GLAZE
Commercial transparent.

DECORATION
Cobalt sulfate on bisque.

FIRING
Gas kiln, cone 14 to 15 (2490°F to 2607°F/1366°C to 1431°C) reduction.

Piet Stockmans, *100 Vases*, cone 14 to 15 porcelain, 39" x 39".

FRITZ ROSSMAN

GERMANY

Blue-and-white porcelain and blue-and-white earthenware have a long tradition in many countries. I am most impressed with the glazework of the Chinese Sung dynasty oxbloods and celadons and the blue-and-white porcelains of the Ming dynasty. I like to express these in a contemporary way, in my own way, to play with the possibilities and to exploit the characteristics that evolve as I work with clay. I use these intuitive discoveries to enhance my forms and surfaces.

The plates are cut out from slabs made on a slab roller, then dropped onto plaster molds to refine the shapes. Handles are handbuilt or cut.

The blue-and-black line drawings are incised in the clay and inlaid with the colored porcelain. This method lends the surface depth, while the working process allows me freedom. The plates are made for daily use, so this glaze must be primarily functional. Petalite gives it strength and clarity. The glaze is both aesthetically pleasing and pleasant to touch.

Some of my work is with crusty engobes and unglazed clay surfaces. These plates are a recent departure. I like the crisp line definition, the fun of drawing and the slightly askew forms, as opposed to my thrown forms.

CLAY BODY
Commercial porcelain body.

Variations

Blue: add 3% cobalt blue stain to dry clay.

Black: add 6% black stain to dry clay.

GLAZE
Clear: petalite 47%, wollastonite 15%, talc 8%, bone ash 4.5%, china clay 19%, silica 6.5%.

FIRING
Gas kiln, cone 10 (2381°F/1305°C) reduction.

Fritz Rossman, *Serving Plates,* cone 10 inlaid porcelain serving plates, 9" x 9" and 13" x 13". Photo by Foto Baumann.

ROBERT PULLEY

UNITED STATES

All my sculpture is built from fat coils that are pinched up. I work from sketches and maquettes, and I work on four to six pieces at a time. When a form is completed, I may select places to burnish and other places to texture. After bisque firing to cone 05, the work is stained with a sponged-on mixture of copper carbonate mixed with a bit of china clay. This surface is wiped down some with a sponge, and glazes are sprayed on. In good reduction the Pulley's Matt will turn mauve from the sponged copper. The Shino gives areas of wonderful orange. The colored matt glazes go well with unglazed passages of clay.

I use an atomizer spray gun with small cups of glaze so I can work rapidly and intuitively. I blend colors, bleed out to raw clay, and accent edges and forms with improvisational ease. I use color to reinforce and accent the planes. Firing is to cone 8 reduction in a gas kiln.

These ceramic sculptures can be installed indoors or outdoors. Indoors they may be bolted to a base or pedestal. Outdoors they will withstand the hardest winters and are their most beautiful in the changing sunlight in relation to trees, plants, stones, sky and earth.

CLAY BODY

Handbuilding clay body:
Goldart 30%, AP Green fireclay 25%, ball clay 10%, potash feldspar 20%, silica 15%. Add 10% sand, 10% grog.

GLAZES

Walt's Shino: nepheline syenite 40%, spodumene 30%, soda ash 8%, ball clay 17%, china clay 5%.

Pulley's Satin Matt: nepheline syenite 28%, potash feldspar 25%, whiting 25%, spodumene 5%, china clay 9%, silica 8%.

Variations

Dark Brown: add 6% rutile, 4% manganese dioxide, 2% chrome oxide.

Ivy Green: add 5% Mason stain 6223.

Pink: add 6% Mason stain 6020.

FIRING

Gas kiln, cone 8 (2305°F/1263°C) reduction.

Robert Pulley, *Broad Shoulder Guardian,* cone 8 stoneware sculpture, 46" x 32" x 16".
Photo by Robert Pulley.

RAY MEEKER

SOUTH INDIA

I became interested in fish as a motif for painting on pots when I saw a Mohenjodaro bowl from the third century B.C. at the National Museum in Delhi. Swimming around the side of the bowl was the most extraordinary pair of fish painted in an iron-bearing slip. The totem is a form that I used many years ago. The vase-cruciform, with a vaguely anthropomorphic trunk, is swathed in thick White Crackle slip that flashes to an intense red-orange in a wood fire where wax has resisted the thin layer of glaze.

The wood fire takes 18 to 20 hours. The colors, especially that violent red, are of tribal essence and give a feel to the shape.

This is a piece of contrast and contradiction, a cloying beauty on a somewhat sinister form with a variety of cultural undercurrents vying for expression. There is nothing esoteric about the clay, slip or glaze used on this vase. It is intensely and unapologetically clay, glaze and fire, serving well the earthy precedents it recalls. It works well with flowers.

CLAY BODY
Stoneware: china clay 25%, ball clay 25%, fireclay 15%, red surface clay 15%, feldspar 7.5%, silica 12.5%. Add 3% sand.

GLAZE
Potash feldspar 40%, rice husk ash 21%, soft wood ash 13%, whiting 5%, siliceous ball clay 22%.

ENGOBES
Iron slip: above body, plus 25% red iron oxide.

White Crackle slip: prospected china clay 80%, potash feldspar 20%.

FIRING
Wood-fired, cone 9 to 10 (2336°F to 2381°F/1280°C to1305°C) reduction.

Ray Meeker, *Totem Vase*, cone 9 to 10 stoneware, 15" high.

BAI MING

CHINA

I am a painter, but so are most Chinese ceramic artists. My artworks are mainly created and fired in the traditional materials of the ancient Jingdezhen village where southern Chinese celadons and oxbloods began in the Sung dynasty, about 900 A.D.

The decorating techniques are far from the simple transplantation of traditional Chinese paintings. My work embodies the integrity and vision of porcelain at different angles. I paint on the clay neither realistically nor abstractly; it is a rather Oriental image of artist conception. I use handmade Chinese brushes with my ceramic engobes against the porcelain bisque — as if it were watercolor paper— and then dip with the clear glaze.

I usually add other ingredients to the traditional ones and play around with the application of brush strokes and water with the pigments for subtle change of colors. It was very difficult to describe the ingredients in English and the percentages, because we don't think so much about the local materials. We are fortunate in China to have access to natural ingredients that have been tested so much in centuries of time. We are taught by tradition. Now I am teaching in the Central Academy of Art and Design in Beijing, where we are using more modern methods.

CLAY BODY
Jingdezhen porcelain.

GLAZES
Base glaze: feldspar, glaze frit, talc, dolomite, straw ash, Chenwan (a local china clay).

Variations
Blue: cobalt, chrome, manganese, iron, copper.

Red: copper, glaze ash, white glass, Chenwan clay.

FIRING
Traditional wood-fired climbing kiln, cone 10 (2381°F/ 1305°C) reduction.

Bai Ming, *Vase with Red and Blue Painting,*
cone 10 porcelain, 11" x 9".

GREG DALY

AUSTRALIA

I am totally over the top with intensity of color, and I love the contrast of copper reds, blues and greens. Each glaze has a strength so it could stand alone, but when combined with other like-intensity glazes, there is terrific contrast and yet balance. When these surfaces are viewed in direct sunlight they drink in the light to reveal depth of color and other colors deep within.

My work is thrown in a very smooth, fine-grained porcelain clay. For bowls like this one, I bisque fire and then spray on the first red at least 0.08 inch (2 millimeters) thick, and up to 0.2 inch (5 millimeters) thick. Hot wax is used to mask out the area to be decorated, then the second red glaze is painted onto the surface as thick as cream. Then an area is masked and the blue glaze painted in, then the green glaze, then the last red glaze — each waxed off between. When finished the overall glaze coat is about 0.3 inch (7 millimeters) thick. Application is very important to color results.

Firing is the key. I begin reduction at about cone 013 and continue throughout the fire. From cone 9 to cone 10 should take one to one and one-half hours in a natural soak. I unpack the kiln the next day; fiber kilns cool pretty fast.

CLAY BODY

Commercial fine white porcelain.

GLAZES

Red glazes: nepheline syenite 35%, whiting 15%, frit (4110 or 3110) 17%, zinc 2%, bone ash 1%, talc 3%, silica 27%.

Variations

First Red: add 1.5% copper carbonate, 1.5% tin oxide.

Second Red: add 1.5% copper carbonate, 1.5% tin oxide, 3% titanium dioxide.

Blue: potash feldspar 63%, whiting 12%, talc 10%, silica 10%, china clay 5%. Add 10% zinc oxide, 2% cobalt carbonate.

Green: potash feldspar 63%, whiting 12%, talc 10%, silica 10%, china clay 5%. Add 1.5% chrome oxide, 0.5% cobalt carbonate.

Last Red: nepheline syenite 44%, frit (4110 or 3110) 13%, whiting 14%, silica 25%, china clay 3%. Add 1% tin oxide, 0.5% copper carbonate.

FIRING

Fiber gas kiln, cone 10 (2381°F/1305°C) reduction.

Greg Daly, *Purple Bowl,* cone 9 to 10 porcelain, 18" diameter. Photo by Russel Baader.

SEQUOIA MILLER

UNITED STATES

My pieces are thrown on an old wooden kick wheel with a fiberglass flywheel. I paddle them when they are soft leather hard. For my flask bottles, I add feet after paddling, four little coils that I cut with a knife to enhance their irregularity. I pulled two little handles off the pot for the ears.

For me, an expressive and varied Shino glaze is the foundation of a glaze palette. I love Shino because it speaks to me, fundamentally, in the language of pottery. It looks like clay in its total range. It enhances the feeling of clayness. It changes color depending largely on thickness and transitions in form. Drips and spots speak to the glazing process itself, like how I held the piece as the glaze dried on it.

I dip the Shino glaze inside and outside. I use a handmade elk-hair brush and commercial black underglaze for the lines, and usually I sponge on the green glaze.

I apply wood ash to the surface; most of it falls on the shoulder as the piece goes into the kiln. Firing Shino is tricky; lots of people have different ideas. I fire my gas kiln in ten hours after a preheat. I close the damper at about cone 06, four-and-a-half hours into the firing, and continue light reduction to cone 11 at 3 o'clock. The kiln cools in 24 hours.

Shino is like water: clear and direct. The overall feeling is serene, but tense and engaging.

CLAY BODY

Commercial iron-rich stoneware.

GLAZES

Werts Shino: nepheline syenite 50%, soda feldspar 15%, spodumene 12%, soda ash 3%, ball clay 17%, china clay 3%.

Willy Hillux Green: nepheline syenite 43%, whiting 21%, china clay 12%, silica 24%. Add 0.75% copper carbonate, 3.75% copper oxide.

FIRING

Gas kiln, cone 11 (2399°F/1315°C) reduction.

Continued on page 100

Sequoia Miller, *Flask Bottle*, 1999, cone 11 stoneware, 5" x 5" x 2". Photo by Tom Holt.

Sequoia Miller, *Oyster Jar,* 1999, cone 11 four-sided stoneware jar, 13" x 9" x 9". Photo by Tom Holt.

ALTERNATIVE SURFACES

Greg Payce

Tjok Dessauvage

Jim Behan

Jeff Oestreich

Randy Johnston

Janet Mansfield

Mindy Moore

Barbara Nanning

Bruce Bangert

Rick Berman

Joan Takayama Ogawa

Matthew Castle

GREG PACE

CANADA

I am not sure I make a true terra sigillata, but I get a nice surface that does not have to be buffed to shine. These recipes are based on Christine Federighi's. I weigh out the components and put them in a large jar mill with lots of balls. I use enough water to make a slurry so the balls move easily, and add the rest after milling. I mill one or two days: the longer, the more sigillata. Then I let it sit two days, pour off the top water and boil the sigillata down until it is the desired thickness. I throw out the sludge.

For tans and reds, I use red or buff clays. For bright sigillatas, I use stains and a ball clay base. I follow a very laborious process that gives consistent results. Stains are heavy and not finely ground. I mix a very large batch of a ball clay that fires fairly white, then dry the sig and break it into lumps. Weigh this and add the percent of stain you want. Put this back in the mill jar and ball mill for 24 hours.

The large vases in the *Apparently* installation were thrown in pieces, joined and turned with a template. They were flicked with thick slip and sprayed with black sigillata, then banded with colored sigillatas. After they dried for a month, they were once-fired to cone 04. Terra sigillata makes a vitreous coating like a glaze, but it is a clay and will not stick to kiln shelves.

CLAY BODY

Jim Smith Red earthenware: prospected red clay 85%, ball clay 10%, talc 5%. Add 0.25% red iron oxide.

TERRA SIGILLATA

White sigillata: water 80%, ball clay 20%. Add 1% Darvan.

Red sigillata: water 80%, Redart clay 20%. Add 1% Darvan.

Black sigillata: water 80%, Redart clay 20%. Add 1% Darvan, 2% cobalt oxide, 1% black copper oxide, 1% manganese dioxide.

Orange sigillata: water 80%, Jordan clay 20%. Add 1% Darvan.

Navy sigillata: water 80%, ball clay 20%. Add 1% Darvan, 2% black copper oxide, 1% cobalt oxide, 1% manganese dioxide.

FIRING

Electric or gas kiln, cone 04 (1940°F/1060°C) oxidation.

Greg Payce, *Apparently,* 1999, cone 04 earthenware pieces with terra sigillata slips, 60" x 36" x 12". Photo by Mark Hutchinson.

TJOK DESSAUVAGE

BELGIUM

The clay I use for terra sigillata is white firing, low in calcium and high in alumina — very fine grained and plastic. It's mixed with water and sodium silicate (a deflocculant), and sieved through a 200-mesh screen. After it settles for one or two weeks, you can distinguish three separate layers in a glass jar. The upper third is the good sigillata and can be decanted. If the process is repeated, the solution becomes finer and can develop a crackled pattern post-reduction, such as you see on this sculpture.

I use a number of firing methods for surfaces similar to those on *Meeting*. Here are several.

1) After bisque fire, place the pot in a closed sagger on a generous one-third inch of sawdust; fire to cone 022 in a gas kiln for an evenly reduced black surface.

2) Wood fire to cone 08 to 04 in oxidation, cool, then reduce heavily from cone 015 to 022.

3) Regular sawdust or pit firings.

4) Gas kiln reduction to cone 08 to 04 with a white clay body gives dense black; a red clay body will yield broken reds against the black.

5) Mix sulfates of various metals (copper sulfate, iron sulfate and others) with the sigillata for color, or add sulfates in sawdust or pit firing for flashing.

Terra sigillata is not a glaze but a very thin, refined clay slip. Overfired, it becomes a glaze. I like the smooth-stone quality of my surfaces against highly polished areas and my incised drawings. The whole has a mysterious feel and a range between light absorbing and light reflecting.

CLAY BODY
Prospected fine-grained clay.

TERRA SIGILLATA
Prospected white clay.

FIRING
Electric or gas to cone 08 to 04 (1751°F to 1940°F/955°C to 1060°C), refire in smoke, closed sagger.

Tjok Dessauvage, *Meeting,* from the *Potstructure* series, 1999, cone 08 to 04 matt and polished terra sigillata, smoke-fired black, 20" x 5".
Photo by Hans Vuylsteke.

JIM BEHAN

IRELAND

throw all my work — usually for salting — and bisque in a programmable electric kiln before the wood fire. I have no formal pottery training so I am not used to intellectualizing what I do. I choose my materials with an eye to retaining the elemental qualities of clay and fire. Wood ash, salt, prospected clays, and stones seem to give me more in this regard.

I decorate mainly by impressing, incising and faceting. Sometimes I alter the wheel form. I don't produce a standard line; all my pieces are "one-off." I need the element of unpredictability. This jar was covered in a manganese cobalt slip that brings out the orange peel of the heavy salting over the finger marks of throwing and the stamped design.

I fire for 18 hours in the wood-burning kiln. Common dry salt is blown into the fireboxes with a sandblaster, the salting beginning as cone 8 goes over. Eleven pounds (five kilos) were used in this firing, for about 60 cubic feet of stacking space. The fireboxes are completely open to maximize fly ash. This pot was positioned on the firebox side of the shelf, where it picked up a good deal of ash, resulting in the pleasing runs of glaze.

There is nothing like opening the kiln after a few days of cooling. I love the excitement of seeing what the capricious fire and glaze have done to my work.

CLAY BODY
Stoneware.

GLAZE
Salt glaze.

ENGOBE
Ball clay from Devon, UK 60%, china clay 40%. Add 2% cobalt carbonate, 12% manganese dioxide.

FIRING
Wood-burning salt kiln, cone 10 (2381°F/1305°C) reduction.

Jim Behan, untitled, cone 10 salt-fired stoneware jar, 8" x 6". Photo by Thomas Sunderland.

JEFF OESTREICH

UNITED STATES

For ten years I fired with wood using glazes that captured the fly ash, and flashing slips. Then I replaced the wood kiln with a soda kiln. I chose soda because the orange peel was more varied against raw clay. I also wanted glazes that would take the soda; matts seemed more suitable, and copper-bearing glazes were in order. Where the soda hits the edges and rims there is a fluxing action and the glaze becomes shiny. The record of the firing process is important.

Along with using soda, I began to stamp into wet clay using patterns influenced by Art Deco details and wax-resist patterns that are geometric and hard edged. I have attempted to take an old German process of salt glazing and use it in my own personal way.

This teapot is thrown and altered by faceting. Glaze is applied by dipping, and the piece is fired in my soda kiln. Heavy reduction begins at cone 010 for a half hour, then a mild reduction until cone 9 is over. Two pounds of soda ash is dissolved in one gallon of hot water. The temperature is held at cone 9 while the solution is sprayed in, which takes a half hour. The ware represents the nature of the fire and yields a record of the firing. This copper-blue glaze sometimes exhibits red accents.

CLAY BODY
Soda-Firing body: #6 Tile china clay 18%, Helmer kaolin 10%, AP Green fireclay 18%, Kentucky stoneware 11%, ball clay 16%, soda feldspar 16%, 325-mesh silica 7%, 48-mesh grog 4%.

GLAZE
Val's Blue-Black: Cornwall Stone 46%, whiting 34%, china clay 20%. Add 4% copper carbonate, 4% tin oxide.

FIRING
Soda kiln, cone 9 (2336°F/1280°C).

Jeff Oestreich, *Teapot,* cone 9 soda-fired teapot with copper glaze, 9" x 9" x 6". Photo by Jeff Oestreich.

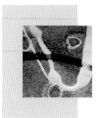

RANDY JOHNSTON

UNITED STATES

Our kiln is an old Bizen-style *noborigama* (climbing chamber kiln). The firebox is built into the structure of the first chamber and allows the ash to be carried directly onto the work from the wood. The kiln is tall: 6'3" from the floor to the inside of the top of the arch. The apex of the arch is set slightly to the rear of the kiln, causing the flame to break into turbulence, facilitating reduction. I learned this from a kiln-building crew in Mashiko, Japan, the village of Shoji Hamada and Tatsuzo Shimaoka.

This bisqued square plate was dipped in the flashing slip. I hesitate to call it a glaze, but it is similar. It flashes to intense red and orange. I learned the glaze ladle-trailing technique used with the black and white glazes from Shimaoka and Hamada in 1975. These glazes are mixed to a thick consistency and trailed onto the piece with a round-lipped ladle.

The fire is started in the mouth of the kiln with oak and maintained for 48 hours in oxidation to about 1000°F (580°C). Stoking above the grate begins the reduction cycle at cone 012. Reduction and oxidation alternate each stoke for the duration of the firing. The second chamber finishes quickly at the end of the third day because of the superheated air coming into the firebox for combustion.

Vitreous slip-glazes for wood fire are any combination of feldspars, nepheline syenite, and clay or mixtures of clays that promotes interesting color from flashing. Free silica added to various mixtures tends to bleach out red colors, so this material is kept to a minimum. We continue to make line-blend tests of clay-flux combinations. I like to use soda-containing fluxes and fine-mesh sizes of high-alumina fireclays with iron impurities, as they seem to offer choices of dramatic color.

CLAY BODY
Stoneware.

GLAZES
Johnston Flashing Slip (for bisque ware): Avery or other china clay 50%, nepheline syenite 50%.

Johnston Trailing White: potash feldspar 43.39%, whiting 10.10%, prospected red clay 2.69%, china clay 8.62%, calcined china clay 8.62%, silica 16.84%, tin oxide 4.87%, Zircopax 4.87%.

Variation
Johnston Trailing Black: add 5.5% Mason stain 6600.

FIRING
Wood kiln, 60 hours, oxidation and reduction cycles.

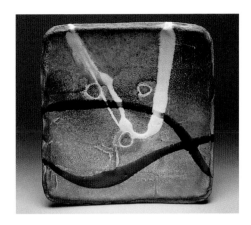

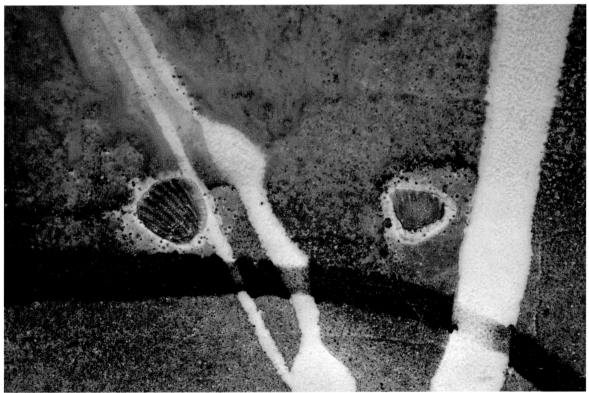

Randy Johnston, *Square Plate,* 1999, wood-fired stoneware, 12" x 12".

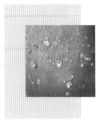

JANET MANSFIELD

AUSTRALIA

I formulate the clay body myself, prospecting the local materials on my sheep ranch in central Australia. Mostly, the glaze and the various patinas result from ash being deposited on the ware during the wood firing. I also make a glaze from prospected materials, which I apply leather hard for another sympathetic surface. It becomes lustrous with a heavy reduction.

I often further decorate the pieces with a china clay slip mixture, casually brushed on, of 80% white clay and 20% local feldspar. Scratches through the slip make marks that will be accented by the firing.

I have nine kilns at Gulgong: one large salt kiln, an updraft gas kiln and several *anagamas* (a single-chamber climbing kiln), including an anagama car kiln built by Fred Olsen in the shape of a car. This vase was fired in one of the anagamas, with wood cut on our place, for three days — about 80 hours.

We have had a number of wood-fire conferences at the ranch. People come from all over the world; we make the pots together, live and cook together, and fire together. There is something truly wondrous about the physical act of firing with wood, the continuous stoking day and night, the building up of the turbulence, the final flames belching out of the kiln at peak temperature. Then it's quiet when the firing stops and it's several days cooling before we can see. I don't know anything much more fun than a wood firing.

CLAY BODY

Stoneware: 60% mix of prospected white and red clays from Gulgong area, 40% local feldspar. The iron content of the clay is around 0.6%.

GLAZE

Naturally deposited ash, plus a glaze of local feldspar 80%, stoneware clay body (above) 15%, bentonite 5%.

FIRING

Wood-fired kiln, cone 12 (2419°F/1326°C).

Janet Mansfield, untitled vase, cone 10 wood-fired stoneware vase, 14" high.

MINDY MOORE

CANADA

This piece is handbuilt from slabs. The image was drawn in the slabs while still lying flat, before the piece was assembled. After bisque firing, the jar was glazed inside and out with the clear glaze. Tatjana (a painter) and I worked collaboratively on this and many other pieces. Some were painted with glaze stains and sprayed with the clear glaze over, but this one was decorated with pastel oilsticks and sprayed with a ceramic sealant.

My approach to clay is to bring out the life of the clay mainly through the form and perhaps texture. With Tatjana, the forms became background, canvas, to receive her images. Tatjana's paintings tend to be brightly colored, and at first she was only interested in that. But in this jar — because the form was complicated — we agreed on more subtle colors. We agreed pastels would work well.

Initially I told Tatjana that I would not throw pots for her to paint on. Our collaboration would have to be more than that. We have known each other for years and have collaborated for about three years. It is a totally different thing to try working on one piece with another person so that the project stays whole and unified, with some of the personality of both people. We have achieved that, and the work shows some of both of us. I am not sure about the "room temperature" decoration with the ceramic sealant. Of course it won't last forever.

CLAY BODY
Commercial porcelain.

GLAZE
Clear: soda feldspar 40%, frit (3195) 20%, whiting 15%, china clay 10%, silica 15%.

DECORATION
Pastel oilstick and ceramic sealants.

FIRING
Electric kiln, cone 8 (2305°F/1263°C) oxidation.

Mindy Moore (with Tatjana Krizmanic, painter), *Jar in Blue and Green with 4 Lids,* cone 8 porcelain with pastels, 18" x 8" x 11". Photo by Marvin Moore.

BARBARA NANNING

THE NETHERLANDS

throw parts and also handbuild for these outrageously huge sculptures that are assembled and glued together. I feel that there should be a balance and harmony between positive and negative elements, between inner and outer form, between growth and gravity.

I sketch these monumental, stylized flowers on the computer. I use an AutoCAD system, running on a PC equipped with Windows 95 and a RenderStar program. Thanks to the 3-D functions, I obtain good visualization of different views of the object.

Ceramic materials cannot easily produce the vivid colors that I want. I have developed a special technique for covering the surface of my objects, after bisque firing, with several layers of pure pigment mixed with fine sand and fixed onto the clay by means of synthetic resin. It is a very laborious technique of chemical substances — with as many as 30 layers of pigments — and finishing. My color palette is beyond the normal possibilities of the ceramics field.

The *Terra* series includes dish shapes made of ceramic inspired by the raked sand of Buddhist gardens in Japan. The Zen gardens made a big impression on me and had a tremendous impact on my work. I tried to recreate the stillness of these stylized gardens in my shapes. The perfect finish of an object, the absence of anything superfluous, the need to take time to do things properly — these are all elements I brought straight back to my own workshop.

CLAY BODY
Stoneware.

DECORATION
Layered pigments under resin.

FIRING
Electric kiln, cone 10
(2381°F/1305°C) oxidation.

Barbara Nanning, untitled works from the *Terra* series, cone 10 stoneware, 18" x 18" x 24" (top) and 27$^1/_2$" x 25$^1/_2$" x 31$^1/_2$". Photos by Ron Zijlstra.

BRUCE BANGERT

UNITED STATES

Years ago, feeling a need to be well rounded, I studied with Herbert Saunders and with Marguerite Wildenhain. Afterwards, I quickly forgot all but what was essential to get started working.

My work appears to be wood fired, but it isn't. The finish you see is not exactly a glaze, being mostly alumina and clay. I hesitate to call it a glaze, but it can go from snow-white to all of the warm fall colors, depending on the clays in the mixture itself and the clay body on which I apply it.

The firing is important due to the thickness of my work. Usually I once-fire in a 24-hour cycle. Reduction begins at cone 010 on the second day and continues to cone 9, when I begin to spray the soda solution into the kiln. I use three pounds of soda ash to one gallon of water. The amount of soda determines the color of my "wood-fire" finish. Too much will make it glossy, which I don't like. I take draw rings out between cone 7 and cone 11. The last draw ring is pulled about a half hour after the kiln is shut off; this is the ring that best tells the story of how the finish will look.

For the artist, chroma, hue and value are the keyboard of a multi-stringed piano. With his eyes being the hammers, he is left free to contrapuntally strike notes that, to the sensitive person, arouse vibrations in the soul.

CLAY BODY
Stoneware: fireclay 62%, ball clay 15%, grog 7%, Nevada sand 6%, lone grog 10%.

GLAZE
Pseudo Wood-Fire glaze: alumina hydrate 50%, fireclay 30%, ball clay 10%, bentonite 10%, mixed and sieved 100 mesh and thinned to specific gravity 45 to 50 on the hydrometer.

FIRING
Gas kiln, cone 11 (2399°F/1315°C) reduction, soda ash solution added.

Bruce Bangert, *Sioux Pi,* cone 11 soda-fired with pseudo wood-fired appearance, 13$^1/_2$" x 15" x 3$^1/_2$". Photo by Wilson P. Graham.

RICK BERMAN

UNITED STATES

This glaze has an incredible range of colors in the raku fire. The glaze should be applied milk consistency to bisque ware. If it is bumpy after firing it was too thick. The colors can range from deep red to orange to green, turquoise, lime, and yellow, depending on how the pot is smoked and quenched. To me this awesome range of colors is best on a simple, round, bulb shape.

The method of firing and post-fire smoking is crucial; you can take notes to duplicate results. I usually fire to cone 04 to 02, hotter than most raku firings. My raku glaze does not bubble during the fire. When the glaze on the pot looks like ice melting, remove it from the fire and set it into a large nest of shredded paper. Do not cover. After 30 seconds, dunk it into water or spray it with a hose and cool it enough to touch. If it is too hot and wet and sits out to air dry, the glaze could shiver, so cool it in the water.

Ceramics is a craft, painting and drawing are crafts, weaving is a craft, and so on. Art can emerge from any of these disciplines, but it cannot be made on purpose. The great art systems of the world were invented by a small number of shamans. It happens today in shamanistic personalities like Cezanne, Monet, David Smith, Christo, Louise Nevelson and Peter Voulkos, to name a few. I am convinced that only crafts can be taught. Art comes as a gift from the universe.

CLAY BODY
Commercial raku clay.

GLAZE
Rick's Turquoise: Gerstley borate 33%, nepheline syenite 17%, spodumene 17%, lithium carbonate 17%, Zircopax 16%. Add 2.2% copper carbonate.

FIRING
Raku kiln, cone 04 to 02 (1940 to 2048°F/1060 to 1120°C), post-firing reduction.

Rick Berman, untitled, 1999, raku-fired globe-shaped jar, 10" x 10" x 10".
Photo by Bart Kasten.

JOAN TAKAYAMA OGAWA

UNITED STATES

The teapot towers are combinations of thrown and cast parts joined together with slip made from the clay body and bisqued to cone 08. Then I use the Otis engobe and paint or spray commercial underglaze colors. Some surfaces are latexed or masked off with graphic design tape, which must be removed before firing. Then the work is glazed with the clear transparent and fired to cone 05 to 04 slowly, for 15 to 20 hours, to prevent pinholes and blisters.

Next I use china paints, which can be fired at cone 019 to 015. Testing and record keeping are vital. I fire several times, the highest-firing colors first, then the lower-firing ones. Gold can be the final firing or it can be layered, but it should not be fired above cone 019. I use a gold pen for fine lines. After the first gold firing I polish with 000 steel wool to buff the surface, then I apply more gold and fire again. I wear medical latex gloves and keep a fan going or work outside.

I use a lot of color theory in planning patterns. I think about light and dark values. I glaze to enhance the form: glaze follows forms. Handles and spouts are glazed similarly to show a connection between the two.

I leave the kiln door open several inches while firing gold, until I can see the gold. Then I close the door but leave the spy-holes out during the rest of the cone 019 fire. This can last as long as 8 to 12 hours, and after all these firings the piece may just crack.

CLAY BODY
Commercial white low-fire clay.

GLAZE
Joan's Transparent: frit (3403) 58%, nepheline syenite 15%, Gerstley borate 15%, lithium carbonate 1%, china clay 3%, silica 8%.

ENGOBE
Otis Vitreous: frit (3110) 20%, Ajax cleaning powder 25%, talc 15%, ball clay 15%, china clay 5%, silica 20%.

DECORATION
Commercial overglazes and underglazes from various manufacturers, including china paints from Matthey-Bishop, luster and gold (Liquid Bright Gold or N Gold) from Hanovia.

FIRING
Electric kiln, cone 019 to 05 (1261°F to 1915°F/683°C to 1046°C) oxidation.

Joan Takayama Ogawa, *Tea Towers,* cone 05 with china paints, lusters and gold, 12" x 12" x 12" (left); 18" x 12" x 12" (center); 14" x 8¹/₂" x 12" (right). Photo by Steve Ogawa.

MATTHEW CASTLE

UNITED STATES

Doubtless many who read this book will be looking at these juicy glazes, one after another, imagining them on their pots. This work of mine is a description of that very process. Also I find it provocative to see a fleeting surface on a pottery object that is associated with permanence, such as a teapot.

There isn't a strong correlation between the projections and the glazes I use for real. When I tried to mimic glazes too closely and was projecting slides against my work for ideas, the projected surface was invariably more striking. I found that for me the projections were best left to be their own thing.

So I made an exhibition about it. I set a projector to advance automatically every few seconds from slide to slide (80 slides in all) and projected these slides onto a bisqued teapot. The photographs here show some stills from this process. This was a piece in and of itself.

For me the exhibition was the best use of the idea of projection. For others, it may be that they can derive ideas from my process. I can see how this process could easily motivate a number of reactions. Someone may want, for instance, to draw inspiration from seeing how varied pictures of the human form look on their wares, or certain colors, or textures. The projected image contrasts with the permanence we think of in ceramics.

CLAY BODY
Stoneware.

GLAZE
Slides projected onto bisque.

FIRING
Virtual glazes are projected on bisqued teapot, cone 04 (1940°F/1060°C) oxidation.

Continued on page 126

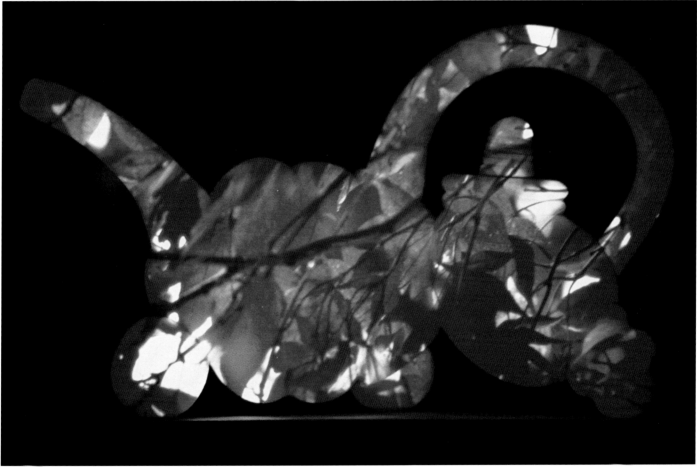

Matthew Castle, *Virtual Glazes,* projected onto a cone 04 bisqued teapot, 6" x 12" x 5"; top photo: stoneware teapot, glazed and fired to cone 10. Photos by Matthew Castle.

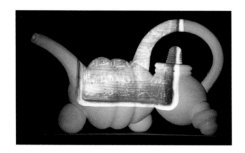  

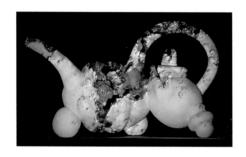 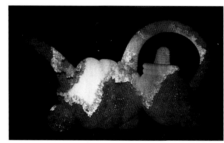 

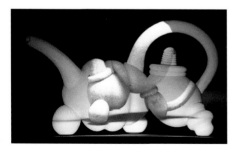 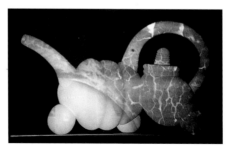 

Matthew Castle, *Virtual Glazes,* projected onto a cone 04 bisqued teapot. Photos by Matthew Castle.

GLOSSARY

Body – A combination of natural clays and ceramic materials specially formulated to give certain workability and firing characteristics.

Bonfire – A method for firing pots in the open; bonfires may reach temperatures of 1300°F (704°C).

Crawling – The property of a glaze to "ball up" into lumps during firing, leaving exposed clay areas. The degree of crawling is determined by the glaze composition and the thickness of application.

Crazing – Cracking of the glaze coat due to uneven contraction between glaze and body during firing.

Dunting – The cracking or breaking of ware due to sudden change in temperature on cooling or faulty clay body and/or glaze composition.

Engobe – A colored clay coating used for decorative purposes. Although an engobe may contain glaze materials, it is not a glaze. However, it may become more vitreous than the body it covers.

Feldspar – An aluminosilicate mineral formed from decomposed granite or igneous rock. Feldspars have soda, potassium or calcium predominant in addition to alumina and silica. They begin melting around 2150°F (1177°C) and – because of their high alumina content – resist running.

Flux – A material that lowers the melting point of something else.

Frit – A commercially manufactured combination of ceramic materials, prefired and reground to produce a nontoxic, chemically reliable, insoluble, low-melting mixture.

Gerstley borate – A substitute for colemanite, this mineral contains calcium, boron, soda and silica, and is useful as a flux at all temperatures. Some batches in *Smashing Glazes* call for Gerstley borate, which is no longer mined. Several ceramic suppliers have developed substitute mixtures. As with any altered glaze, testing is the best way to arrive at a substitute batch that will work for you.

Glaze binder – Materials used in solution with the glaze batch to protect the surface or keep the glaze in suspension. As little as 1% CMC gum, gum arabic or gum tragacanth can be added to the glaze batch, dry or liquid. Binders in solution with water can be used as protective sprays on raw majolica decorations.

Gloss – A shiny glaze.

High fire – Kiln temperatures in the highest range for functional and sculptural ceramics, from about cone 8 (2305°F/1263°C) to cone 14 (2491°F/1366°C); produces stoneware and porcelain.

Ione grog – A refractory grog with good thermal shock resistance.

Low fire – Kiln temperatures from 1300°F (704°C) up, but usually considered to be cone 010 to cone 04, or 1641°F (894°C) to 1940°F (1060°C); produces earthenware.

Matt – A glaze surface that is not shiny. Matt glazes range from dry to dull to stony.

Medium fire – Kiln temperatures in the mid range, usually considered to be cone 03 (2014°F/1101°C) to cone 6 (2232°F/1222°C); produces stoneware.

Opaque – A material that will not allow light to pass through. Opaque glazes obscure any decoration when the glaze is of normal application. Opacifiers are tin oxide and zirconium compounds such as Zircopax, Superpax and Opax.

Oxidation – A kiln firing atmosphere with enough air for complete combustion.

Oxide – A chemical element combined with oxygen. In ceramics, "oxide" also refers to the coloring oxides of metals that withstand temperatures above red heat, such as copper, cobalt, iron, manganese and vanadium.

Percentage – The part of a whole expressed in hundredths. Ingredients in a glaze are written in percentages to enable comparisons; the sum of all the ingredients in the base equals approximately 100.

Porous – In ceramic terms, a clay body that leaks or absorbs water after firing. Porous bodies are more fragile than vitreous bodies.

Pyrometric cone – A commercially manufactured, elongated, pyramidal-shaped object about 2 inches high, made of ceramic materials calculated to melt as an indicator of heat work. Each cone formulation is given a number to indicate the specific temperature at which it will soften and bend. There are several cone manufacturers – all with slightly different temperature equivalents. Orton is the standard for the United States, Seger for Europe. Cone numbers begin around 022 (Orton: 1086°F/586°C) diminish to 01 (2079°F/1137°C), and then increase again from cone 1 (2109°F/1154°C) to cone 42 (3659°F/2015°C).

Raku – A method of low-temperature firing. Glazed or unglazed ware is placed into a hot kiln and pulled out minutes later, then either air cooled, quenched or smoked in organic material or newspaper.

Raw – Unfired clay or glaze.

Reduction – A kiln atmosphere of reduced oxygen, which changes oxide colors in clay bodies and glazes: notably, copper oxide, which in oxidation is grass green, in reduction Chinese red; small percentages of iron oxide produce amber to yellow in oxidation and celadon green in reduction.

Refractory – A material that resists heat and melts at a very high temperature.

Sagger – A clay container in which pottery is stacked to protect it from flames during firing, or a container for holding fuming material such as metallic oxides, chemical salts and organic substances that act on ware during firing.

Salt glaze – A method of glazing ceramics by introducing common salt (NaCl) into a hot kiln nearing the maturing temperature of the ware, often yielding an "orange peel" texture.

Shivering – The cracking off of fired glaze, usually on rims or edges, due to compression. Shivering may occur during cooling or weeks later.

Slip – Any liquid mixture of clays and water, including casting slip for molded pieces and liquid colored clay engobes.

Soda vapor glaze – A method similar to salt glazing, in which soda ash (sodium carbonate) is used rather than salt.

Suspension agent – A material that retards settling in the glaze or slip batch, such as Epsom salts (magnesium sulfate), Macaloid, bentonite or Veegum T and its variants.

Texture – Surface variations in clay or glaze can be carved, applied, inlaid or created by the addition of coarse particles that remain after firing, or by the addition of combustible particles (like coffee grounds or sawdust) that burn out, leaving voids.

Translucent – A material that lets light pass through, such as thin porcelain; a slightly clear glaze, shiny or matt.

Transparent – A clear, glasslike glaze.

Vitreous – A clay body fired sufficiently to be hard, durable, leak proof and sanitary.